Rx *for* WORRY:

A THANKFUL HEART

JAMES P. GILLS, M.D.

CREATION
HOUSE
PRESS

RX FOR WORRY: A THANKFUL HEART
by James P. Gills, M.D.
Published by Creation House Press
A Part of Strang Communications Company
600 Rinehart Road
Lake Mary, FL 32746
www.creationhouse.com

Unless otherwise noted, the Scripture quotations are
from The Holy Bible, New International Version,
© 1973, 1978, 1984 by the International Bible
Society. Used by permission of Zondervan
Publishing House. All rights reserved.

Excerpts from the book, *Future Grace*, by John Piper;
Multnomah Publishers, Inc., copyright 1995.
Used by permission.

Cover design by Debbie Lewis
Interior design by David Bilby

Library of Congress Control Number: 2002107031
International Standard Book Number: 0-88419-932-0

400,000 copies in print

04 05 06 07 — 8 7 6 5 4 3 2
Printed in the United States of America

To all those who struggle in the war against worry, I dedicate this book. May each of us find peace by resting and rejoicing in the promises of God.

Acknowledgments

This book could not have been written without my good friend and colleague, Gary Carter. Gary's insight, wisdom and sense of God's joy have guided us through countless discussions about the thorny issues of worry and faith. He has been an invaluable partner in prayer and praise throughout the writing of this book.

I am also deeply grateful to the staff members at St. Luke's Cataract and Laser Institute for their support and timely words of encouragement. Special thanks go to Lois Babcock for her commitment to this project. And I owe much to the patients at St. Luke's, who have shown me valuable lessons in trust.

My wife, Heather, continues to be a source of strength and support. Her love, rooted in the love of God, is an inspiration to me.

Contents

INTRODUCTION

In my practice as an ophthalmologist, we say that the worst part of cataract surgery is the week before the actual procedure. That's when patients really start to think about the procedure and anticipate its effects. Many patients get concerned at this point about whether the surgery will hurt or whether they will lose their vision. And if they previously had a bad experience with some other procedure, they will be afraid of the cataract surgery.

These concerns and fears are very important and very real. A patient's attitude affects his ability to relax and cooperate with us during surgery so we can do the best possible job. Therefore, it is essential that we help a patient understand the procedure, and that we provide as much comfort and reassurance as possible.

But for some people, it doesn't matter how much support we offer. Some patients are going to worry about all aspects of their lives. They're paralyzed by their worries, and they can't enjoy life.

Do you know someone who has been paralyzed by fear and negative thinking? Or have you personally ever been so worried that you couldn't think clearly, couldn't sleep peacefully, couldn't act wisely? This kind of chronic worry is a highly infectious disease that can permeate our inner being. It can infect our thoughts, attitudes and actions. It can destroy us physically and emotionally. Worst of all, it can destroy us spiritually, because chronic worry drives a wedge between us and God.

When we're ruled by worry, we don't have complete trust and faith in God. We don't think we can depend on Him. We feel isolated and alone. We blame God for all the bad circumstances in our lives, and we fail to see the blessings He provides.

THE TREATMENT FOR WORRY

Fortunately, we can banish fear and worry. I've seen the treatment work time and again in the lives of my patients. They have shown me that a constant attitude of thanksgiving breaks the grip of fear. These patients, in addition to facing their own surgery, may have family members who are dying; they may have financial problems; or they may be struggling in a personal relationship. They're certainly sad at times as they grapple with the problems in their lives, but they're not worried. They're thankful for God, and they continually feel His presence. They are thankful for all of the ways He provides for them, including the surgery that will help them. Because of their faith, they can look beyond their struggles and see God at work. They have the same concerns and problems any of us face, but they choose not to worry. They choose to be thankful.

They live the words of the apostle Paul:

> *Rejoice in the Lord always. I will say it again: Rejoice! Let your gentleness be evident to all. The Lord is near. Do not be anxious about anything, but in everything, by prayer and petition, with thanksgiving, present your requests to God. And the peace of God, which transcends all understanding, will guard your hearts and your minds in Christ Jesus.*
>
> —PHILIPPIANS 4:4–7

Paul tells us that the thankful spirit is the basis for all of life. He tells us to not worry, but to always be thankful to the Lord. Just like these patients, we can reject worry. We can rejoice with thanksgiving. When we're focused on the person of Jesus Christ in thanksgiving, our anxieties and fears can be wiped away. Our hearts can overflow with a spirit of peace and joy because He lives in us.

What a relief to know that each of us can turn to God and put our lives in His hands! We can be thankful for His blessings and let thanksgiving fill our hearts. We can be filled with peace regardless of our circumstances. We can be faithful to the one who faithfully provides. We must focus on Him with thankful hearts.

Are you weighed down with worry? Are you filled with fear? There's refuge in the loving arms of God. He will break the bonds of worry. He will banish fear. We get His real and lasting peace when we turn to Him and say, "Thank you, Father, for always loving me. Thank you for the eternity that you have given me through the person of Jesus Christ, who died and rose again for me." When we turn to Him, no longer will we fear and worry.

> *Do not let your hearts be troubled. Trust in God; trust also in me. Peace I leave with you; my peace I give you. I do not give to you as the world gives. Do not let your hearts be troubled and do not be afraid.*
> —JOHN 14:1, 27

Certainly none of us can avoid the situations and circumstances that can create worry and fear. But we can avoid the worry itself by having a spirit of thanksgiving. We can turn to God and trust in His goodness. We can choose His peace rather than the troubles of this world.

In this book, let's explore ways to build our trust in God, deepen our faith, practice a spirit of thanksgiving and take practical steps to win the war against worry. The discussion questions at the end of each chapter are designed to help you examine the fears and worries in your life and look at ways you can strengthen your own relationship with God. You may also use the questions as part of a group study, to help you talk about real issues within a Christian setting. The discussions also include additional Scripture verses to provide further insight.

In addition to a bibliography and a scripture index, this book includes one additional appendix: a section called "Putting Promises into Action." God's Word, the Bible, is full of His promises about how He will take care of us. This index lists His promises about specific issues and circumstances. When one issue weighs you down, you can turn here to read His promises and use these verses in the fight against fear.

Do not fear, for I am with you.

—ISAIAH 41:10

The Bible tells us repeatedly to "fear not." Many of those passages are followed by the words "I am with you." It is because God is with us that we do not need to fear. He will always be with us. May we learn to trust fully in God, with thanksgiving for His grace. He will destroy fear and worry! He will give us peace! Now and forever! Amen!

CHAPTER 1

THE
WORRY
DISEASE

A few years ago I got this new sports car. It was just perfect. I loved the color and the model. And it came with all kinds of electronic extras and gizmos. It was the fanciest car in the world. But there was one problem. The brake constantly locked on one wheel. Every time I accelerated, I would spin around in circles.

While this isn't a true story, it does illustrate how worry affects us as human beings. Worry puts a brake on one of our wheels. We may be the sharpest sports car in the world, but we will only go around in circles if worry consumes us.

Let me confess that I've spent a few sleepless nights worrying about my job, my wife, my children. I know some people who, when they worry, have trouble eating. Others shut themselves up in their offices or homes. In their isolation, worry strangles them. Worry takes its toll in many areas of our lives. Let's look at some of its damaging effects.

INTELLECT

When our thought processes are cluttered with worry, we can't have creative and energetic ideas. We produce sloppy and inaccurate work. We focus more on the pressure that deadlines create rather than on the quality of our work. And if we have trouble eating or sleeping, it becomes even more difficult to focus our minds. We can't process information and decide what's important, so we're disorganized. We can't decide which plans to follow, and we are unproductive. We're distracted; we jump from one task to another and never have a feeling of completion. We become indecisive; we fear making the wrong decision so much that we can't make any decisions. We can become workaholics, driven by worries about job or financial security.

EMOTIONS

Our worries produce an uneasiness in us which causes us to be *irritable* and susceptible to *panic attacks*. "Where did we park the car at the mall? Where are my glasses? Where is that pen? Where did I put that bill which is due today?" We also can be *depressed, negative, critical, judgmental, domineering* and *controlling*. We isolate ourselves and end up *lonely*. We might be able to force others to be around us, but they don't do it willingly because we're no fun to be with. In addition, worry stifles our ability to reach out to others. We don't want to let our guard down and trust others, so worry locks us up in a *life of isolation*. We get involved with fewer and fewer people and groups. We have problems building genuine friendships. Our emotions seem *out of control*, and we do not respond normally to everyday situations.

HEALTH

Worry is a progressive disease that can ruin our lives, and even kill us. Worry depletes us and has tangible effects on our health. It may even cause us to have *hypertension*. It sometimes destroys our ability to fight against diseases by decreasing our natural immunity. Our decreased immunity permits common *colds* to strike us, and, if our immune system breaks down further, worry may even permit us to be stricken by more serious diseases. Certainly anxiety is the basis of many *psychiatric diseases* and psychosomatic diseases. Charles Mayo, co-founder of the Mayo Clinic, pointed out how worry affects the body. It affects the circulatory system, the heart, the glands and the nervous system, to name just a few. Mayo used to say that he never knew of anybody who died of overwork, but he did know people who died of worry.[1]

So we can *worry ourselves to death*, but we can never worry ourselves into a longer, healthier, happier life.

Now let's look at the benefits of a thankful life focused on God.

When we're filled with a spirit of thanksgiving, we are at peace with God. And when we have His peace, we're at peace with ourselves and others. We're productive at work, accomplishing a great deal more, because we can focus on the task at hand. We can eat properly, rest properly and heal properly. We have harmonious relationships with our family and friends. We're able to love and serve others, forgive them, be thankful for them, encourage them and appreciate them. Our lives are filled with thanksgiving.

The chart on pages 4 and 5, using God's Word, shows the difference between the mindset of worry and the mindset of peace and thanksgiving.

Chronic worry creates anxiety and stress in our lives. It destroys our relationship with God and other people. We accuse others, judge others, discourage others and try to control others. We're negative people who don't feel God's love and can't love others. But when we have a thankful spirit, God's peace and love fill our lives. Our focus is on His eternal presence and blessings. We are positive, trusting, loving, supportive and appreciative.

The attitudes of two sisters named Mary and Martha illustrate this difference between persons who worry and those who don't.

Jesus and His disciples stopped at the sisters' house to visit and

WORRY	THANKSGIVING
But the worries of this life, the deceitfulness of wealth and the desires for other things come in and choke the word, making it unfruitful. —MARK 4:19 (Worry keeps us from listening to God.)	*I will listen to what God the LORD will say; he promises peace to his people.* —PSALM 85:8 (We listen to God.)
If you keep on biting and devouring each other, watch out or you will be destroyed by each other. —GALATIANS 5:15 (Worry causes poor relationships.)	*Let the peace of Christ rule in your hearts, since as members of one body you were called to peace. And be thankful.* —COLOSSIANS 3:15 (We have peaceful relationships.)
The way of peace they do not know. —ROMANS 3:17 (Worry destroys peace.)	*You will keep in perfect peace him whose mind is steadfast, because he trusts in you.* —ISAIAH 26:3 (We have internal peace.)
Cursed is the one who trusts in man . . . he will be like a bush in the wastelands. —JEREMIAH 17:5–6 (Worry dries us up spiritually.)	*The eternal God is your refuge, and underneath are the everlasting arms.* —DEUTERONOMY 33:27 (We feel God's provision.)
The seed that fell among thorns stands for those who hear, but as they go on their way they are choked by life's worries . . . and they do not mature. —LUKE 8:14 (Worry makes us unproductive in our work for the Lord and otherwise.)	*Trust in the LORD with all your heart and lean not on your own understanding; in all your ways acknowledge him, and he will make your paths straight.* —PROVERBS 3:5–6 (We are productive under God's guidance.)

WORRY	THANKSGIVING
"Martha, Martha," the Lord answered, "you are worried and upset about many things." —LUKE 10:41 (We are frazzled in our work.)	*Trust in the Lord . . . Delight yourself in the Lord . . . Commit your way to the Lord . . . Be still before the Lord and wait patiently for him.* —PSALM 37:3–7 (We have peace in our work.)
Do not love the world or anything in the world . . . The world and its desires pass away, but the man who does the will of God lives forever. —1 JOHN 2:15, 17 (We're focused on the material world.)	*Though outwardly we are wasting away, yet inwardly we are being renewed day by day.* —2 CORINTHIANS 4:16 (We're focused on eternity.)
Their father Jacob said to them, "You have deprived me of my children. Joseph is no more and Simeon is no more, and now you want to take Benjamin. Everything is against me!" —GENESIS 42:36 (We miss God's purpose.)	*And we know that in all things God works for the good of those who love him, who have been called according to his purpose.* —ROMANS 8:28 (We know God is in control.)
I have no refuge; no one cares for my life. —PSALM 142:4 (We feel alone and isolated. We don't sense God's presence.)	*So do not fear, for I am with you; do not be dismayed, for I am your God.* —ISAIAH 41:10 (God is with us.)

eat. While Martha scurried around the house getting everything ready for the meal, Mary sat at Jesus' feet and listened to Him talk. Finally Martha was so irritated about doing all the work by herself that she complained to Jesus. "Lord, don't you care that my sister has left me to do the work by myself? Tell her to help me!" Jesus' words probably surprised her: "Martha, Martha, you are worried and upset about many things, but only one thing is needed. Mary has chosen what is better, and it will not be taken away from her" (Luke 10:40–42).

The problem wasn't that Martha was working. The problem was her attitude. Martha wasn't thankful that the Lord had come to visit with her. She was worried about the burden it created—fixing a meal, preparing the house, tending to the guests. Jesus told her to change her focus. Rather than giving priority to her work, she needed to give priority to God. Jesus praised Mary for her attitude. She knew the most important thing wasn't what she did. It was that she was thankful for the presence of the Lord and was aligned with Him.

It's the same with each of us. Jesus sees through our work and worry. He knows that what we really need is to change our focus. When we give priority to tangible actions and results, such as our work, we'll be filled with anxieties and fears. But when we're aligned with Him, those worries vanish. We're filled with thanksgiving for His presence in our lives. We see the way He guides our lives and blesses us. We're totally committed to Him. As a result, we're engulfed with the presence of God through the person of Jesus Christ.

Which lifestyle would you choose? Would you rather be engulfed with the God of peace or paralyzed by worry?

The choice seems clear. But it isn't always easy. Worry can sneak up on us. Satan knows that, given the choice, we'd rather have peace than the turmoil that worry creates. So he uses our own weak human will and desires to lure us into a lifestyle of worry. Worry starts innocently enough, I think, as a normal, natural concern about our basic needs. Do we have enough money to buy adequate food, clothes and shelter? Is our health good? Are our friends and family healthy and happy?

It is perfectly natural to have these concerns. In fact, it's good that we are concerned, because then we're moved to action. We work so we can afford food and clothes and shelter. We go to the doctor when we don't feel well. We try to be loving and thoughtful to our family and friends. And we are thankful to God for all He provides.

But Satan uses the values of the world—tangible goods we can see, hold and measure—to lure us away from our trust in God. As we become less God-centered and more self-centered, our concerns become worries. We quit trusting that God will provide adequate food and clothes. We believe that we need the right clothes, the right house, the right car, the right job, the right spouse, the right country club. We think we have to take care of ourselves, and we worry about circumstances and events beyond our control. We can become selfish, and then we don't trust others because we assume they're selfish also. We worry about irrelevant and inconsequential concerns, such as whether there's enough money in the parking meter. We're overcome with negative thoughts, and can't tell the difference between legitimate concerns and problems that exist only in our heads.

Worry has us firmly in its grip. And it's happened to all of us at some point in our lives. None of us is immune from selfishness and the worry that it creates.

> *We all, like sheep, have gone astray, each of us has turned to his own way; and the LORD has laid on him the iniquity of us all.*
>
> —ISAIAH 53:6

This verse is a great motivation for me. First, I see myself going my own way, acting on my own dreams, aspirations and desires. Then, I see Christ on the cross, bearing my sins. In the first scene, I'm enjoying my sinful pleasure and not caring about God. In the other scene, Christ is caring about me and bearing the penalty for my sins.

Two effects result from my visualization of this verse. First, it breaks my heart and challenges me. Second, it provides strength of motivation to know that He loves me to that degree. It binds my heart to Him so much that I want to be loyal to Him. I begin again to trust in God with my whole heart, and put aside my selfish ways to seek His will.

Will you do that with me now? Pray with me:

> Lord, I am selfish. I have let you down. Forgive me when I try to live by worldly standards. Forgive me for thinking that I can't depend on you. I commit myself again to seeking your will and not the ways of the world. I know that I am your child and that you will take care of me. Thank you for your endless fountains of love, mercy and grace. Thank you for the strength that comes from trusting in you. Amen.

There's good news for us sinners. Worry isn't permanent! In the next few chapters, let's look more closely at the forms selfishness takes and the different ways it creates worry. We'll also see God's plan for combating selfishness and surrendering to His will.

DISCUSSION QUESTIONS

1. What are you worried about now? How is it affecting your health? How is it affecting your relationships?

    _____

    _____

    _____

2. What makes you feel peaceful? How does that attitude affect your health and relationships?

    _____

    _____

    _____

3. List some ways to practice being thankful this week. For example, say "thank you" to someone you encounter today—a sales clerk, a receptionist, a neighbor. Or write a note to someone special.

    _____

    _____

    _____

4. What are some of your obstacles to asking God for His peace?

    _____

    _____

    _____

5. What scripture speaks to your heart about your
    worries?

_____

_____

_____

For further reflection:

Search me, O God, and know my heart;
*   test me and know my anxious thoughts.*
See if there is any offensive way in me,
*   and lead me in the way everlasting.*

—PSALM 139:23–24

The writer of this psalm is asking for true intimacy with God.
Ask God to explore your own heart and help you wipe away any
anxious thoughts that might be there.

CHAPTER 2

A
NEW
PERSPECTIVE

Worry comes from the Old English term *wyrgan*, which means to choke or strangle.[2] Worry can creep into our lives and strangle us. Jesus says in Mark 4:19, "The worries of this life, the deceitfulness of wealth and the desires for other things come in and choke the word, making it unfruitful."

Each of us is tempted by the desires of the world. For some, it's clothes or cars. For others, it's a relationship or a career. All of us battle those selfish desires to see, measure and own the tangible possessions of the world.

Do you worry about keeping your possessions, your health, your status or position in life? Jesus tells us to change our focus.

> *Do not store up for yourselves treasures on earth, where moth and rust destroy, and where thieves break in and steal. But store up for yourselves treasures in heaven, where moth and rust do not destroy, and where thieves do not break in and steal. For where your treasure is, there your heart will be also.*
>
> —MATTHEW 6:19–21

Jesus tells us to not concern ourselves too much with earthly goods. We should be more concerned, He says, about eternal treasures. When we look at this world through eyes focused on the eternal God, we see His blessings. We don't care whether we have more material possessions. We do care about loving and serving God with thanksgiving every day, and about letting that love guide our actions with others. Being aligned with God helps us care for others—a sure antidote to selfishness.

It's natural to be concerned about having adequate food, shelter and clothes. But when worldly values creep into our thinking, we've chosen earthly treasures. We've chosen to turn our backs on His Word, creating a void in our lives. The world tell us the way to fill the void is by getting more—from our profession, our relationships, our appearance, our status in life, our money and our possessions.

So we worry about keeping what we have and about getting more. We worry about whether we can trust others, because we think everybody is just looking out for themselves. We worry about making the right impression on the right people so they'll think we are important. We find ourselves feeling we need to own places, people and possessions, and we worry about whether we can keep them. We thought we would be free when we had enough money, friends, power and influence. We thought we could "have it all," and now all of it has us. We're spinning around struggling to maintain our lifestyle.

Now, where are our treasures?

God wants to give us a new vision of life. Think of it as our Father owning the land on both sides of the river. One side is the present; the other side is eternity. We will be eternally cared for by Him. There is nothing we could want that He can't provide. Freedom from want frees us from worry. We have no fears of loss or even death. He has promised to let us live in His presence forever. We have the freedom of that eternal bliss of being engulfed with Him.

So we fix our eyes not on what is seen, but on what is unseen. For what is seen is temporary, but what is unseen is eternal.

—2 Corinthians 4:18

Earthly treasures are fleeting. Living in the presence of God lasts for eternity. Thanks be to God for the eternity we have with Him!

Let me share with you a story about a man who was engulfed by the eternal presence of God. Martyn Lloyd-Jones, a former physician, served as minister of London's Westminster Chapel for 30 years and was widely regarded as a powerful British preacher. As he grew older and weaker and worn, near his death in 1981, his doctor said to him, "I don't like to see you so weary and worn and sad like this." "No," he said. "Not sad."[3] And he wasn't. He knew he had nothing to fear. He knew he had the kingdom of God. He would spend eternity with his Creator, Redeemer and Sustainer.

Do not be afraid, little flock, for your Father has been pleased to give you the kingdom.

—Luke 12:32

Our Father has given us His kingdom. Of no importance are the jobs we have or the possessions we own. Of great importance are the eternal matters—such as our home with God in heaven. Our earthly possessions are His blessings, and we should praise Him for giving us such gifts. But our true home, our true security, is found in the person of Jesus Christ. Being a member of His kingdom gives us a place, beginning now and lasting through eternity.

Martin Luther said, "I live as though Jesus died yesterday, He rose today and is coming back again tomorrow."[4]

Think of Jesus as dying only yesterday. Calvary was yesterday. The power of the resurrection was yesterday. The power we live by today is the Holy Spirit. We live with Jesus today.

Tomorrow, we look forward to His grace for eternity.

> *Therefore, I tell you, do not worry about your life, what you will eat or drink; or about your body, what you will wear. Is not life more important than food, and the body more important than clothes? Look at the birds of the air; they do not sow or reap or store away in barns, and yet your heavenly Father feeds them. Are you not much more valuable than they? Who of you by worrying can add a single hour to his life?*
>
> *And why do you worry about clothes? See how the lilies of the field grow. They do not labor or spin. Yet I tell you that not even Solomon in all his splendor was dressed like one of these. If that is how God clothes the grass of the field, which is here today and tomorrow is thrown into the fire, will he not much more clothe you, O you of little faith? So do not worry, saying, "What shall we eat?" or "What shall we drink?" or "What shall we wear?" For the pagans run after all these things, and your heavenly Father knows that you need them. But seek first his kingdom and his righteousness, and all these things will be given to you as well.*
>
> —MATTHEW 6:25–33

In these verses, Jesus is explicit in His instruction to not worry. He puts our concerns in proper perspective. We are of much greater value than the birds and flowers that God takes care of. We have nothing to fear because the Lord knows what we need and He will give it to us, now and for eternity.

Jesus wants us to be free from the worries and anxieties that can rule our daily lives. He wants us to see our lives from God's point of view, not man's. He wants us to see the world around us as short-lived, our problems as temporary. He wants us to take our focus off our own needs and desires and plans; that's thinking by the standards of this world. Instead, He wants us to focus on eternity in His presence. God will take care of our problems; all we need to do is rest in His presence. When we understand that, how can we worry about the events and circumstances of this world? We have all of eternity with Christ stretching out before us.

Dietrich Bonhoeffer, as he faced execution by the Germans during World War II, said, "This is the end, but also the beginning."[5] Each of us can live with the anticipation of heaven in our hearts. His presence is relevant to our daily lives—our jobs, our relationships, our mental thoughts and attitudes, our rising in the morning and resting at night, and our continual thanksgiving for that eternity.

This eternal perspective has practical applications. Let's look at five steps each of us can take to diagnose and analyze our worries.

1. **Take one day at a time.** "This is the day the Lord has made; let us rejoice and be glad in it" (Ps. 118:24). We are often so busy smothering the present moment with worries about tomorrow or regrets about yesterday that we kill today. Don't worry about tomorrow or six months from now. Don't worry if the government is going to take over the medical system or if Social Security is going to go broke. We just need to do the very best we can, where we are, with what we have. Don't worry about the rest. Tomorrow belongs to God. We have no control over the future, but He has promised to provide for us eternally. We have only today; let us enjoy it and be thankful.

2. **Get the facts.** Write down all the information you have for the situation you're worried about. Keep a list on paper, not in your head. Not everything comes quickly, but write down all the details and analyze them. "What exactly is it that I'm worried about? What are the consequences? How does it really affect me?" As we write down our worries, we become followers who trust in God to provide and who see Him at work.

3. **Analyze the results.** As we think through a worrisome situation, often we realize it's not the event that troubles

us—it's the anticipation of the event. We realize certain things are going to happen regardless of what we do. Those that can't be cured must be endured. And we can endure them because we know God is in control now and for eternity. Our attitude of thanksgiving will help us put Him first and trust in His goodness and kindness to us.

4. **Improve upon the worst.** Business people always look at a problem by projecting the worst possible scenario. Then they put all their energy into ensuring that the worst won't happen. We can often improve the end result if we take positive steps to prevent the most negative results.

5. **Be done with it.** Put the worry behind you; you've done all you can to take care of the problem. Refuse to allow it to continue bothering you. Give the problem to God, with thanksgiving, and know that He can handle any situation. He is the King of kings and Lord of lords!

In paintings, artists use perspective to portray different views of the same object. As Christians, there is only one perspective we must have—the perspective of eternity. That perspective sets the tone for our lives. All our daily actions can be carried out against the background of eternity. Every decision, every action, every thought, every attitude is based on our eternal life through Christ. We're engulfed by Him and our lives are entwined with Him forever.

DISCUSSION QUESTIONS

1. What material goods do you value? Do you think of them as earthly treasures? Why or why not?

2. What are treasures in heaven? Do you think of
    yourself as having them? List ways this affects your
    daily life.

    _____

    _____

    _____

3. Each of us has a weakness for some material pos-
    session or circumstance. What's yours? How does
    Satan use it to make you worry?

    _____

    _____

    _____

4. Apply the five steps of analyzing worry to one cur-
    rent concern in your life. How does it help?

    _____

    _____

    _____

For further reflection:

For to me, to live is Christ and to die is gain.
—PHILIPPIANS 1:21

Paul writes that everything he does on earth is to glorify the
person of Jesus Christ. And when he dies, he will be with Christ
for eternity. So it makes no difference. If Christ is in everything
we do, we don't have to worry about anything. All we have to do
is rejoice and be thankful. Amen.

CHAPTER 3

WHO'S IN CHARGE?

In the spring of 1980, a series of earthquakes and small eruptions drew the attention of people living in the Pacific Northwest. Scientists and sightseers were drawn to Mount St. Helens. Steam vents, tremors and hot spots appeared almost daily. Then on May 18, a 5.1-magnitude earthquake shook the mountain. For a few seconds the north flank seemed to ripple, then broke loose and began sliding downhill as a massive avalanche. Eruption plumes shot up as quickly as 600 miles an hour. The blast traveled as a hot, churning mass of gas, rock, ash and ice. More than fifty people were killed or reported missing after the blast, and the eruption devastated 235 square miles.[6]

The eruption of Mount St. Helens was a tragedy. It's also a powerful reminder that there are forces in this world over which we have no control. Even when the best scientific minds and equipment were keeping watch over the mountain, they could not predict what was going to happen next. It's the same way in our lives. Despite our best efforts and knowledge and abilities, there are some events and circumstances over which we have no control.

We can't control the stock market, which dictates how well our money might perform. We can't control another person's thoughts and feelings, which dictate how strong our relationships might be. And even if we eat right and exercise regularly, we can't completely control our health. Accidents, disease and illness still happen.

Historian Barbara Tuchman said, "War is the unfolding of miscalculations."[7] Much of what goes on between nations is based upon a struggle for control. When a nation believes it can control another, or when a government thinks it can control its citizens, it miscalculates and wars ensue.

On a personal level, miscalculations can be just as chaotic or devastating. When we act as though we understand and can control events, circumstances and people, we make a huge mistake. Control is another form of selfishness. Trying to control shows that we've replaced our trust in God with faith in ourselves. But that kind of faith always results in failure.

Let's look at the struggle for control another way.

Have you ever spent time with 2-year-olds? Some of their favorite phrases are "mine," "no" and "I do it." They want to be independent. They think they know what they're doing. They have faith in their developing skills and abilities and judgment. Sometimes that streak of independence is frustrating to parents who have to wait as the child struggles to climb in and out of a car seat by himself. Sometimes it is dangerous. No matter how smart or capable a 2-year-old is, he should not play with the stove or try to cross the street by himself.

But children persist in testing the limits of their independence. For instance, there's the little one who uses the kitchen drawers like a ladder to climb up to the counter. Like a kitten caught up in a tree, he gets stuck in a situation he's not equipped to handle. And only then does he start to worry about how he'll get down. Then comes the cry for help.

How often are we like that with God? Have you ever wanted to "do it" yourself rather than wait for Him? What happened? I think all of us are tempted to rely on our own brains and brawn. When we put our faith in ourselves, we lose sight of God's love and care. We're like that 2-year-old climbing onto the kitchen counter. Once we get stuck, we get scared.

> *In my distress I called to the LORD;*
> *I cried to my God for help.*
> *From his temple he heard my voice;*
> *my cry came before him, into his ears.*
> *He brought me out into a spacious place;*
> *he rescued me because he delighted in me.*
>
> —PSALM 18:6, 19

What a consolation to know that a power greater than our-selves can restore us! God wants to keep us safe. He doesn't do it out of a sense of obligation. He does it because He loves us. He delights in caring for us. Not only that, He's told us that He will eternally provide—in this world and the next. He wants us to trust Him to provide.

When we're selfish, we care deeply about how much we have. We try to control what we have and we calculate ways to get more. But if we're trusting in God, we don't care whether we have more or less. We know He will provide for us regardless.

> *Trust in the LORD with all your heart and lean not on your*
> *own understanding; in all your ways acknowledge him, and*
> *he will make your paths straight.*
>
> —PROVERBS 3:5

We have to trust in God and let Him guide us. We have to hand Him our independence and our desire for control. We have to let Him take the reins of our lives in His hands.

Trust is not always easy. We've grown to like the beliefs and values of the world, even if we're filled with worry. We're in the habit of trusting ourselves, not trusting God. We're comfortable with the lifestyle of work and worry that we've developed.

We must let go of worldly attitudes so we can firmly grasp God's hand. Then we can let Him lead us. We can give Him control of our lives, and we can walk in trust and thanksgiving.

> *When I am afraid,*
> *I will trust in you.*
> *In God, whose word I praise,*
> *in God I trust; I will not be afraid.*
> *What can mortal man do to me?*
>
> —PSALM 56:3–4

I memorized this passage years ago. It helps me align myself with God and His Word. It reminds me that God is in control and that I don't need to be afraid or try to be in charge myself. Reciting these verses in times of trouble has helped me worry less and trust more. God's Word can help you, too.

DISCUSSION QUESTIONS

1. What circumstances beyond your control do you worry about? How can you release your desire for control?

_____

_____

_____

2. When are you selfish? When are you reluctant to trust in God's ability to provide?

_____

_____

_____

3.   List some reasons why you can trust God.

_____

_____

_____

4.   Memorize Psalm 56:3–4 this week. Then recite these verses the next time you need encouragement about God's provision. List here how the verses helped.

_____

_____

_____

For further reflection:

> The LORD is near to all who call on him,
>   to all who call on him in truth.
> He fulfills the desires of those who fear him;
>   he hears their cry and saves them.
>
> —PSALM 145:18–19

God is in control of our lives and eternity. We can call on Him and He will save us. Share some examples of how He has done this in your life.

CHAPTER 4

PEACE IN GOD'S PROMISES

"I'm getting gray-haired from worrying."
"Why are you worried?"
"Because I'm getting gray hair."

This fictitious conversation might sound trite, but it shows the destructive cycle worry creates. Once we start to worry about one area of our lives, it becomes easier to worry about another, and soon all we do is worry. Some patients I see are always worrying. I can offer many reassurances and give them all the information they need, yet they still worry. They're in the habit of worrying—about their cataract surgery, about their cars, about everything you could imagine. These folks' first reaction to a problem is worry.

Any of us could let worry become a way of thinking and a way of life. Worry produces more negative thoughts. And negative thoughts produce negative people. I've been around negative people in my life, and I don't like it. I'm sure you've been around them, too. Negative people constantly complain and criticize. Nothing is ever good enough for them.

When worry sets in, we need to condition ourselves to respond in faith, not fear. The best way to replace that bad habit of worry is with a good one—looking to God's promises rather than our own feeble, human solutions. These promises are His own words. He reminds us that He will intervene. He will help us. He will give fresh courage and strength. He will calm the storms in our lives.

> *Taste and see that the* LORD *is good;*
>   *blessed is the man who takes refuge in him.*
> *Fear the* LORD, *you his saints,*
>   *for those who fear him lack nothing.*
> *The lions may grow weak and hungry,*
>   *but those who seek the* LORD *lack no good thing.*
> —PSALM 34:8–10

Throughout the Bible, God promises to provide for us. We should have no doubts, no fears, no worries. We must remember God's pledges and promises to provide, especially in those times when we're tempted to worry rather than to trust in His faithfulness.

THE BLAME GAME

Chronic worriers tend to quit taking responsibility for their actions. As children, they say, "My mother won't let me do this or that," or "The school won't let me do this." As they mature, they continue to find external reasons for their problems. They believe they have no control over the events in their lives, but that other people do. They act like they are pawns or victims.

They look to others for reasons for their own problems, but they don't look to God as the solution for their problems. First they need to see that God loves them and will provide for them. They need to surrender their lives to God, having faith in his eternal promises and grace. Nothing can conquer those who truly believe in Him.

> *We are hard pressed on every side, but not crushed; perplexed,*
> *but not in despair; persecuted, but not abandoned; struck*

down, but not destroyed. We always carry around in our body the death of Jesus, so that the life of Jesus may also be revealed in our body.

—2 CORINTHIANS 4:8–10

They must take these promises and believe that they have the freedom to make positive choices which will benefit them to the glory of God. God has given them the ability to take responsibility for their actions and their lives.

Blame looks to the past, which can't be changed; but responsibility looks to the future—which can be taken care of and managed, through the grace of God.

DO WE MEASURE UP?

There are times in each of our lives when we compare ourselves with others. We might get jealous of the new car our neighbor buys. Someone else in the company gets the promotion we should have had. We wonder whether our children are as successful as the children of our friends.

Jesus talks about this attitude in the parable of the Prodigal Son. Most of the story is about the younger son, who took his inheritance and wasted it all. When the younger son came home, his father welcomed him with open arms and threw a huge party. When the older son heard about the party, he was furious. He thought it was unfair that his father should be so generous with someone the son judged as undeserving.

Look! All these years I've been slaving for you and never disobeyed your orders. Yet you never gave me even a young goat so I could celebrate with my friends. But when this son of yours who has squandered your property with prostitutes comes home, you kill the fattened calf for him!

—LUKE 15:29–30

The older brother wanted his father to be fair. But his father, like any father, was more than fair. He was loving. His response:

My son, you are always with me, and everything I have is
yours. But we had to celebrate and be glad, because this
brother of yours was dead and is alive again; he was lost and
is found.

—LUKE 15:31–32

The father had a greater vision. He loved both of his sons,
and that was more than enough. God is the same way with us.
As much as we might worry or complain about another's suc-
cess, we need to remember that God loves each of us. And His
love for one person doesn't have anything to do with His love
for someone else. All we should do is look to Him.

Do not fret because of evil men
*   or be envious of those who do wrong;*
for like the grass they will soon wither,
*   like green plants they will soon die away.*
Trust in the LORD and do good;
*   dwell in the land and enjoy safe pasture.*
Delight yourself in the LORD
*   and he will give you the desires of you heart.*
Commit your way to the LORD
*   trust in him and he will do this:*
He will make your righteousness shine like the dawn,
*   the justice of your cause like the noonday sun.*
Be still before the LORD and wait patiently for him;
*   do not fret when men succeed in their ways,*
*   when they carry out their wicked schemes.*
Refrain from anger and turn from wrath;
*   do not fret–it leads only to evil.*
For evil men will be cut off,
*   but those who hope in the Lord will inherit the land.*

—PSALM 37:1–9

But it's not just comparing our lives with others that causes
us to worry. We also worry about whether other people like us
and accept us.

As I grew up, I saw young girls whose parents didn't accept

them. They worked out their sexuality in a way that cost them satisfaction in their lives, and they ruined everything by not allowing the Lord to work. They never had peace. They ended up trying to find acceptance in every circumstance and person and place, but not in the Lord.

The desire for acceptance is strong in human nature. If we don't feel the grace of God accepting us, we can act out in many ways to seek acceptance from others. We may be reckless in the way we drive a car or run a business or spend money. We may become belligerent, aggressive or violent, trying to earn others' acceptance and respect. And we may be sexually irresponsible, seeking a false sense of security and love.

If we're busy worrying about what others think of us, we're selfish; we're not aligned with God. Our relationship with the Lord has changed. It's like a relationship with a person to whom we were close but now we're distant. We can't really talk to them; there's no closeness any more. The telephone wires to the Lord seem to be cut down. We do that simply, and I mean very simply, by being critical or envious of others and being worried about how we compare with them.

We're worried about the attitudes of others toward us, rather than our attitude toward God. We need to get back in the good habit of practicing faith and remembering His grace. If God accepts us as the sinners we are, and if He will provide everything we need, why should we be worried about what others think and do?

We should be filling our minds with our relationship with God and spending our time in His presence. We need to realize there is nothing as important as Him and our relationship with Him. This helps us be more free and joyful, less anxious and worried, and less critical and judgmental.

FEAR OF LONELINESS

Alone, alone, all, all alone,
Alone on a wide, wide sea!
And never a saint took pity on
My soul in agony.

—The Rime of the Ancient Mariner
SAMUEL TAYLOR COLERIDGE

Each of us has an inner longing for the eternal God. When it's not filled with a connection with God, we're lonely. Our hearts are seeking something, and the many possessions and jobs and relationships we have tried don't seem to be it. We believe if we just rush around enough, keep busy enough, and surround ourselves with enough important and interesting people, our loneliness will disappear.

We can fear this loneliness, and we try to ignore it by manipulating others to get love and attention from them. Or we try to fill the void by seeking people as possessions, not as genuine relationships. "Loneliness and the feeling of being unwanted is the most terrible poverty," Mother Teresa said.[8] This fear is very dangerous. It causes many people to make bad choices for friends and marriage partners. The fear of not really being loved causes many people to enter into harmful relationships and wrong marriages.

But we are filled only when we give ourselves to Christ in a personal relationship with Him. Loneliness is banished when we are truly connected with the Lord. Then we are able to make divine connections with others through the Holy Spirit.

Another cure for loneliness is friendship with godly friends. These friendships are selective, sacrificial, steadfast and secure. Friendships are special when they are totally committed; when each person is willing to do anything for the other. Lives are no longer empty and lonely. We change who we are. God is working in our friendships to make our lives more meaningful.

THE LURE OF MONEY

People who want to get rich fall into temptation and a trap and into many foolish and harmful desires that plunge men into ruin and destruction. For the love of money is a root of all kinds of evil.

—1 TIMOTHY 6:9–10

Frequently we worry about money. We are in awe of it. It is the world's measuring stick of accomplishments. The world tells us that we will succeed and gain respect if we earn enough money. The world's life is determined by money, money status, money power, money obtained from work, money needed, the fear of not having enough money in the future and the fear of losing the money presently in hand.

We can think about money more than we think about God. We can end up worshiping money and have no time to worship God. Money can displace God from our lives. It becomes our god. I've seen myself, and many other people who are very interested in the Lord, do it. When we're focused on money, we think about it in such a way that we worry and are not at peace.

The deceitfulness of riches is that money promises everything; it appears to give some things, but in reality it gives nothing. In the end, money lets us down. When we worry that we won't have enough money to meet our needs, we're not trusting the Lord to provide. We're forgetting His eternal perspective. We're allowing our fears to control us. The fear of running out can be worse than actually running out.

That worry is more harmful to us than any decreased financial status. It ages us, it changes our judgment, it consumes and controls our lives; it takes us away from God. Money puts us in bondage. How can we worship God on Sunday and cheat on our taxes—or anything else—throughout the week? The mind games we play show that we are devious and not devoted to God. We are being untrue. Money is not worth cheating. We fool ourselves if we think finances are of such great importance.

Our true worth is not measured by having money in the bank; or by having cars and houses. Our true worth was measured on the cross and is reflected by our response in faith and thanksgiving to Jesus' death and resurrection. The cash we live by is the presence of Jesus in our lives.

COUNTING THE COST

Here's a favorite exercise of mine. If I start getting too worried or anxious about a situation, I like to take a step back from it. Maybe I even step up to a mirror, look myself in the face, and ask, "Is this worth the worry?" Jesus poses the same question:

> *Are not five sparrows sold for two pennies? Yet not one of them is forgotten by God. Indeed, the very hairs of your head are all numbered. Don't be afraid; you are worth more than many sparrows.*
>
> —LUKE 12:6–7

God loves us and treasures us as His children. He has everything under control for all eternity. All we need to do is remember to look to Him and let Him provide. Praise be to God for His infinite wisdom and mercy! Amen.

DISCUSSION QUESTIONS

1. Do you know someone who plays "the blame game"? How can knowing 2 Corinthians 4:8–10 help?

_____

_____

_____

2. When have you compared yourself with others?
    How does it help you? How does it hurt you?

    _____

    _____

    _____

3. When have you felt lonely? What helps you out of
    that feeling?

    _____

    _____

    _____

4. What helps you find meaningful relationships with
    others?

    _____

    _____

    _____

5. How important is money to you? Do you think you
    have enough? What does God say about how much
    is enough?

    _____

    _____

    _____

For further reflection:

Set your mind on things above, not on earthly things.
                                    —COLOSSIANS 3:2

The only way to mature in God is to put Him first. List five
ways you can do this in your daily life.

CHAPTER 5

A
PERSONAL
STORY

Through the years I've met many people who have had to battle fear and worry. I'd like to share with you the story of one of my patients. Because of a previous condition with one eye before she came to St. Luke's Cataract and Laser Institute, she was very anxious. She struggled with fear before her eye surgery at St. Luke's, and we spent time discussing the habit of worry and fear she had built up over the years. After her eye surgery, she wrote me this letter detailing her struggles with fear and her victories over worry.

FEAR AND HOW I AM OVERCOMING IT

Dear Dr. Gills,

I have been ruled by a four-letter word all my life—Fear.

I remember being in bed at night when I was 4 or 5 years old and being afraid. I would be afraid to turn my back to the wall, thinking a big witch would come out of the wall and "get me." I remember it very well to this day.

Then I remember being scared by a movie my parents took me to. They let me sleep with them for a few nights, but they got tired of that. They made me walk the living room floor to tire me out so I'd go into my own bedroom. I got tired, but was still scared (it was an awful movie), so I wouldn't give in. I remember crying and crying, and being so tired and feeling I just had to take this punishment and fear. In other words, I was a real victim.

Growing up, and as an adult, I was always afraid of something going wrong or happening to my body. Results of tests and so forth would worry me so. I was not scared of other hardships or disappointments in my life—just my body.

Fear would take me over; I was always imagining the worst. It was not a fear of pain, but a fear of being helpless.

Even the expression on my face would and does become tense and tight, and the body language I'm sure reflects the same. This robbed my energy and made me feel tired all the time.

I had tremendous fears about my eyes after my first retina problem, which was detached. (This was a condition I had before I came to St. Luke's.) I was always afraid of "losing my eyesight." And I just couldn't find a way to handle this.

When I finally knew I had to get my one good eye operated on, I put it off as long as I could, until I couldn't live with that fear any longer and bit the bullet and set the date at St. Luke's.

I was a nervous wreck weeks before, even though I knew I had the best eye doctor in the world. I had utmost confidence in him. It was my eye I was scared of. My daughter gave me advice on one of the two ways I helped myself be less afraid before the surgery. She said, "The day before, get out and work off all that tense energy in your body. Walk and/or swim until you are so tired." I didn't feel like doing that; I was so used to being all tensed up. But I did. And it helped immensely.

But the most important thing: Through prayer I was able to finally "let go," surrender myself to whatever was God's will. I was thinking positively, but knowing and really accepting God's will to be for my best, and it was entirely in His hands.

Of course I can report I came out with better sight than I dreamed of, and with a loving, effortless procedure.

You have to face your fear, not just escape into TV or whatever and take your mind off it. You have to face, accept, and let go. Then fears escape you.

Now I know how much imagination has to do with fear. It's probably the whole thing. Because if you're actually face to face with a fearsome thing, like a lion, you have to do one of two things: run or fight him, and it's over. The worry and fearful thinking whether something could or would happen is really only in our imagination. So why can't we make the choices and substitute that fear-imagination with positive and good results? We must learn tools of how to do just that when the other pops in. Learn and fine-tune them until we only expect the best. This is the task. That is what I really have to learn and use, and I'm sure there are many others who need to also learn these tools.

I'm grateful to share this with you.
Valerie Tourin.

DISCUSSION QUESTIONS

1. The writer of this letter could remember being afraid as a child. What scared you as a young child?

_____

_____

_____

2. What scares you now? Do those fears change your
    behavior?

    _____

    _____

    _____

3. List the tools you can use to face your fears this
    week.

    _____

    _____

    _____

4. Describe an experience in which you applied these
    tools and overcame fear.

    _____

    _____

    _____

For further reflection:

*The LORD himself goes before you and will be with you; he
will never leave you nor forsake you. Do not be afraid; do
not be discouraged.*
                                        —DEUTERONOMY 31:8

God tells us to not be afraid because He is with us. How do
you know God is with you today?

CHAPTER 6

THE WEAPONS AGAINST WORRY

FAITH, GRACE, AND THANKSGIVING

Worry takes root in our lives when our selfish interest keeps us from being aligned with God. When we're selfish, we worry about material, earthly concerns in our lives and in the lives of those around us. We fear events and circumstances beyond our control. And chronic worry will destroy us. When we're worried, we can't think straight, we can't sort out our emotions, we act irrationally and we eventually can kill ourselves with the stress that worry causes.

We need to ask ourselves what worries us. What's putting a brake on our physical, emotional and spiritual health? How long have we had it? Can we release that brake? Can we get rid of the worry? Can we get rid of the selfishness?

Praise God that He has given believers victory through the person of Jesus Christ! Jesus understands our human nature. Far worse than ever being hungry a little bit is worrying about it beforehand. Worse is worrying about having enough money to buy the right clothes. Worse is worrying about being able to live the way we want to live. Jesus knows worry destroys the beautiful peace that comes from God living within us.

He knows there's only one way to break the bonds of worry, and that is through Him. The basic treatment for worry is a life of thanksgiving for God's grace and faith in His provision, all built on the cross of Jesus' sacrifice. We can walk up the gangplank of faith, full of thanksgiving, into the ship of God's grace.

A deeper understanding of faith, grace and thanksgiving, through Christ, can help us defeat worry.

FAITH

There is a story about a fellow from the country, who, after years of avoiding flying, had the thrill of his first airplane trip. He reached his destination and returned safely. Upon his return, a friend asked what he thought about the trip. "Well, to tell you the truth," he said, "I never did put all my weight down on the airplane."

Have you ever done that? There have been times in my own life when I've been reluctant to put all my weight down on Christ. I was just not quite sure I wanted Him to help me through a tough time or predicament. Then the inevitable happened. The situation got far worse than if I had just trusted in the Lord.

This is the opposite of what God wants us to do. He promises He will take care of us; we don't need to worry.

> *I lift up my eyes to the hills—*
> *where does my help come from?*
> *My help comes from the LORD,*
> *the Maker of heaven and earth.*
> *He will not let your foot slip—*
> *he who watches over you will not slumber;*
> *indeed, he who watches over Israel*
> *will neither slumber nor sleep.*
> *The LORD watches over you—*

the LORD is your shade at your right hand;
the sun will not harm you by day,
nor the moon by night.
The LORD will keep you from all harm—
he will watch over your life;
the LORD will watch over your coming and going
both now and forevermore.

—PSALM 121

What beautiful promises! Day and night, He will watch over us. As any father watches over a child, God watches over us. We can put our entire weight on Him; we can have faith in Him. And then we can let our minds be at peace.

There's one biblical account of total faith that always speaks to me. It's the story of a father who was willing to sacrifice what he loved most because he trusted in God.

In Genesis chapter 22, God tells Abraham to take Isaac, his only son, to the land of Moriah and sacrifice him as a burnt offering. Now, this seems like something Abraham wouldn't want to do. He and Sarah had waited so long to have Isaac. Would he want to give him up? What would he tell Sarah? And this act seems contrary to the promise God had made that "it is through Isaac that your offspring will be reckoned" (Gen. 21:12). But Abraham collected the wood for the burnt offering, packed up his donkey, and headed off with Isaac.

When they got close to Mount Moriah, Isaac got curious. He wanted to know where the lamb was for the burnt offering. "God Himself will provide the lamb," (22:8) Abraham said, showing total trust. They got to the place God directed, and Abraham started preparing for the sacrifice. He built the altar and arranged the wood. Then he tied up Isaac and put him on top of the wood. Finally, he pulled out his knife to kill his son. At that moment, the angel of the Lord called out to him:

"Do not lay a hand on the boy," he said. "Do not do any-
thing to him. Now I know that you fear God, because you

have not withheld from me your son, your only son."
—GENESIS 22:12

And then Abraham saw a ram caught in some bushes, and he took it and sacrificed it in place of his son. To this day it is said, "On the mountain of the LORD it will be provided" (Gen. 22:14). A new name was given to this spot, to encourage all believers to cheerfully trust in God: *Jehovah-Jireh*, the Lord will provide.

Abraham's encounter helps me remember that God, as our Father and as our Shepherd, will always provide. Faith is a great weapon against worry. I know He will provide. And I know this not just in my head, but in my heart. I know He's intimately involved in my daily life.

I have been crucified with Christ and I no longer live, but Christ lives in me. The life I live in the body, I live by faith in the Son of God, who loved me and gave himself for me.
—GALATIANS 2:20

Living fully in the kingdom of God is a life of faith. We need to focus on God in all the moments of our days, noticing His work in our lives and appreciating and thanking Him. We do our planning, lay the groundwork, act responsibly and trust God for the results.

Faith is the essence of our strength in the eternal God. Then joy, peace and hope can blossom forth because we know we will be provided for. We can be totally content in Him, because we know we have everything we need through the person of Jesus Christ. George Mueller once said it this way: "Where faith begins, anxiety ends; for where anxiety begins, faith ends."[9]

Life hits us in waves of good events and bad circumstances. These can create anxiety and joy, happiness and fear. Satan would love to use those bad times to undermine our faith. He would love for us to give in to our fears and anxieties. He would love for us to forget God's promises of provision and start to rely on our weak human efforts. He would love for us to worry.

But faith says we're content in our present state. Faith says we have enough, whether we are rich or poor, in good health or sick, young or old. Regardless of circumstances and events, we know our daily strength is in the Lord. The only stability we have is in Jesus Christ. We must stand firm in faith, knowing God provides.

Paul, who was imprisoned many times, shows us we can be happy and content regardless of our circumstances because we have faith in Christ. Locked in prison, Paul still rejoiced because his joy was in Christ, not in external circumstances.

> *I am not saying this because I am in need, for I have learned to be content whatever the circumstances. I know what it is to be in need, and I know what it is to have plenty. I have learned the secret of being content in any and every situation, whether well fed or hungry, whether living in plenty or in want.*
> —Philippians 4:11–12

What a testimony of faith! Like Abraham, Paul knew the Lord as his *Jehovah-Jireh*—his provider. He saw the circumstances in his life from an eternal perspective. He had an unshakable faith in the person of Jesus Christ. And he knew the abundance of God's grace, that God loved him so much He would always sustain him.

Paul and Abraham show us that we don't need to be afraid. When our "treasure" is with God, with faith in Him, this world can do nothing to truly harm us. We are reassured in this life by our knowledge and belief in eternal life in the person of Jesus Christ. We belong to the Creator, Redeemer and Sustainer of the universe. We are His children and He will protect us and provide for us. We don't need to worry. We have nothing to fear. The Lord will take care of us now and for eternity.

GRACE

Why does God love such selfish, rebellious, independent people as you and me? Why does He love us even though we worry and fret and complain? Because of His grace. This grace is totally undeserved. We haven't done, and we never will do, anything to earn it. We can never show that we have earned His grace. We can only show that we don't deserve it.

> *For it is by grace you have been saved, through faith–and this not from yourselves, it is the gift of God–not by works, so that no one can boast.*
> —EPHESIANS 2:8–9

By the grace of God, we are what we are. It is by His grace that we are saved. Everything is done by the grace of God, and by the grace of God we allow others to be who they are. We just have to get it through our heads, our hearts, our pride and our sense of self-importance, that His grace allows Him to love us and provide for us beyond our understanding.

Here's an example: A man arrived in heaven and was asked, "Do you have your thousand points?" He told all about the good he had done—going to church, helping others, being true to his wife and working hard. The response was, "That isn't worth a thousand points; that isn't being as good as Christ." Then another man arrived. His answer was, "I have no points. I have no worth on my own. The only thing I have is Christ Himself." That person was accepted into heaven.

Our actions and accomplishments do not save us; focusing on the person of Christ and the cross saves us. Praise God for His grace! For if we were treated fairly, if we were given what we deserved, none of us would be spending eternity with our Creator, Redeemer and Sustainer.

All worry and fear are knocked out when we believe in this grace. When we let God's grace be the ruling aspect of our lives, fear and worry leave. When grace is present, we become indifferent. We surrender to His will and feel His firm fingers of control over our lives.

We're filled with joy because we know we're with Him forever and He will provide for us forever. We realize the power of the resurrection is ours for eternity. Author John Piper calls it "future grace"—grace which is ours not just after our entrance into heaven, but which fills each moment as God provides for us.[10] His grace is sufficient for today, tomorrow and eternity.

We can use our faith in His future grace to battle worry in practical ways. Piper, the pastor of Bethlehem Baptist Church in Minneapolis, encourages us to look to God's promises when fear and anxiety try to take hold in our lives. God's promises are His own words. He will intervene. He will help us. He will sustain us. He will give us fresh courage and faith.

Here are some examples Piper uses in his book about the subject, *Future Grace*.

When we're anxious about a new situation and **fear the unknown**:

> So do not fear, for I am with you; do not be dismayed, for I am your God. I will strengthen you and help you; I will uphold you with my righteous right hand.
>
> —ISAIAH 41:10

When we're anxious about our efforts to serve God and we **feel useless** and empty:

> So is my word that goes out from my mouth: It will not return to me empty, but will accomplish what I desire and achieve the purpose for which I sent it.
>
> —ISAIAH 55:11

When we're anxious about the **weaknesses** we feel in our lives:

> My grace is sufficient for you, for my power is made perfect in weakness.
>
> —2 CORINTHIANS 12:9

When we're anxious about decisions that will affect our

future:

> *I will instruct you and teach you in the way you should go;*
> *I will counsel you and watch over you.*
>
> —PSALM 32:8

When we face **opposition**:

> *If God is for us, who can be against us?*
>
> —ROMANS 8:31

When we're anxious about the welfare of **family and friends**, we can remember that God is our father and knows how to give good things to His children:

> *If you, then, though you are evil, know how to give good gifts*
> *to your children, how much more will your Father in heaven*
> *give good gifts to those who ask him!*
>
> —MATTHEW 7:11

When we're anxious about being **sick**:

> *A righteous man may have many troubles, but the* LORD
> *delivers him from them all.*
>
> —PSALM 34:19

When we're anxious about **aging** and getting old:

> *Even to your old age and gray hairs I am he, and I am he*
> *who will sustain you.*
>
> —ISAIAH 46:4

Future grace doesn't just keep us from needing to worry—it demolishes worry! The beauty of God's future grace is that it will be sufficient not only now, but for eternity. We are His forever. His provision is forever. God gives us future grace with such hope that nothing else should cause us to worry today. We're intertwined and engulfed with Him forever and He'll provide for us forever. His Word will reassure us of His promises and strengthen our belief in His future grace. If we don't realize the beauty of God's future grace to take care of us forever, then we have failed to realize the purpose of the creation and our purpose in living. That purpose is to have a state of peace, to glorify God and enjoy Him forever because we rest in His grace.

THANKSGIVING

Banks Anderson, a doctor in ophthalmology at Duke, was once asked, "If you had only one medicine, what would you take?" He said, "Steroids, of course. They can treat many ophthalmologic diseases; more than any other medicine." Steroids can knock down inflammation and treat more diseases than any one antibiotic or immunosuppressant agent.

As I think about the therapy for worry, I think of the best medicine—the thanksgiving frenzy to the Lord. This attitude of thanksgiving is more than something we do at meals, at birthdays, at holidays. It's a mental attitude of continual thanks to God that permeates our thoughts and lives. It engulfs our relationship with God, our relationships with others and our relationship with our vocation. It's a daily necessity in the war against worry. Philippians 4 tells us how important thanksgiving is.

> *Rejoice in the Lord always. I will say it again: Rejoice! Let your gentleness be evident to all. The Lord is near. Do not be anxious about anything, but in everything, by prayer and petition, with thanksgiving, present your requests to God. And the peace of God, which transcends all understanding, will guard your hearts and your minds in Christ Jesus.*
>
> —PHILIPPIANS 4:4–7

Paul is talking about a habit and lifestyle of thanksgiving—a thanksgiving frenzy. He tells us we are to give thanks in all things. We are to be prayerful in all things. The two really fit together. Because when we give thanks, we are thankful to our Creator, our God. We pray prayers of thanksgiving.

A spirit of thanksgiving is not an optional attitude for us. If we are to experience a true relationship with God, we must be thankful to Him. We're thankful for the grace that saves us from our sins. We overflow with thanksgiving for the person of Jesus Christ living in us. He takes away our sin and accepts our repentance.

A thankful heart is the basis of a healthy heart—a heart that is holding onto Him. We must be thankful for God's grace—His future grace and His past grace. We have the future grace of being intertwined with Him for eternity. What joy we will have being with Him and our loved ones for eternity! It's this joy that changes our lives. It's this thankfulness for our future that keeps us walking in the Spirit.

Being thankful to Him takes us from despair. Being thankful to Him takes us from being perplexed and crushed. Being thankful to Him gives us a joyous, happy and overcoming heart. We're thankful from the top of our heads to the bottom of our feet. We can praise the Lord in the midst of difficult times because we have seen His blessings in the good times. We can ask God, listen to Him, pray for deliverance and seek His wisdom.

Some of us say the words "thank you" so often that they become a part of us. Others are quiet and express "thank you" with a touch, a look, an attitude of care and concern—understanding and appreciating without words. We're all different, and we're thankful that we are. But each of us must express our spirit of thanksgiving.

Luke describes how one man demonstrated the thankful spirit:

> Now on his way to Jerusalem, Jesus traveled along the border between Samaria and Galilee. As he was going into a village, ten men who had leprosy met him. They stood at a distance and called out in a loud voice, "Jesus, Master, have pity on us!"

> When he saw them, he said, "Go, show yourselves to the priests." And as they went, they were cleansed.

One of them, when he saw he was healed, came back, praising God in a loud voice. He threw himself at Jesus' feet and thanked him—and he was a Samaritan.

Jesus asked, "Were not all ten cleansed? Where are the other nine? Was no one found to return and give praise to God except this foreigner?" Then he said to him, "Rise and go; your faith has made you well."

—LUKE 17:11–19

One man came back to Jesus in thanksgiving. One related to Him. One became personal with Christ. This is the thankful state each of us should have. We must give ourselves to God in thanksgiving and live on a person-to-person basis with Him, because the Holy Spirit lives within us. This thanksgiving frenzy aligns us to God.

Being thankful helps us to realize who God is and who we are. We stand in thankfulness because of His constant forgiveness of our constant sins and rebellion against Him. Indeed, we cannot give thanks until we realize that we are nothing on our own, yet everything through Him. We know His future grace, His present grace and His past grace will take care of us. It is truly impossible to worry if we are in a thanksgiving frenzy.

Through Jesus, therefore, let us continually offer to God a sacrifice of praise—the fruit of lips that confess his name.

—HEBREWS 13:15

It is impossible to be in a state of worry if we are in a thanksgiving frenzy. In thanksgiving, we are focused on God in the person of Jesus Christ, and we're thankful for everything we have. Thanksgiving banishes selfishness—the seeds of worry. It's impossible to focus on ourselves if we're continually thankful to God for being our provider now and forever. This eternal view puts worry in its proper perspective. A thanksgiving frenzy lifts our life above the cares of this world. We know what is real, lasting and true. We are thankful to God for His presence and eternity with Him. Thanksgiving gives us the peace of God rather than the anxiety and fear generated by the concerns of this world.

A thankful spirit extends beyond our relationship with God. It also strengthens our relationships with our loved ones. A thankful spirit is so essential in many relationships, especially that of marriage. Steadfast thankfulness produces strength, support and growth in marriage. Continuous gestures of love, support and thanks give our spouse a sense of self-worth; they build a relationship of trust and love.

In the same way, we need to be thankful for other friends, family and co-workers—all those with whom we rub shoulders in our daily lives. We can serve, we can give, we can be partners, we can love others when we have a genuine spirit of thanksgiving for them.

This spirit must be the essence of everything we do. In every activity, whether it's doing delicate surgery or writing books or presenting a legal defense or sweeping a hall, we must have an attitude of thanksgiving.

> Give thanks to the LORD, call on his name;
>   make known among the nations what he has done.
> Sing to him, sing praise to him;
>   tell of all his wonderful acts.
> Glory in his holy name;
>   let the hearts of those who seek the LORD rejoice.
> Look to the LORD and his strength;
>   seek his face always.
>   —PSALM 105:1–4

My only really outstanding athletic achievement was a Double Iron Triathlon in which I finished about one minute behind the first American competitor in the event. At the time, I was 56, and he was 28. Both of us did very well. But what's interesting is that for me, the most important thing I did was to stay in an attitude of thanksgiving during the whole race.

In that race I never had the up and down cycles most athletes usually face in long competitions. Instead, I concentrated on reciting Bible verses and being thankful. I never really struggled. There was no effort. The attitude of thanksgiving permeated everything I did during that race.

Being thankful moves our faith to rest in His grace. Faith, grace and thanksgiving, embodied in the person of Jesus Christ, take away our need to worry and allow us to be engulfed by the presence of God—now and for eternity. That is the ultimate antidote for worry!

THANKSGIVING AND LAUGHTER

We can take thanksgiving one step further. When we're filled with thanksgiving, we're joyful. It's impossible to be gloomy and depressed when our hearts are full of thanksgiving to God. This thanksgiving frenzy manifests itself in a way we don't always consider: laughing.

How long has it been since you had a good belly laugh? Good laughter seems to be a treasure that is in short supply. It is one of the gifts of being human, and it is an essential ingredient in life. Many times as we try to clear our minds of different thoughts, desires and wants, we should just simply look at the situation and start laughing. Laughter, particularly as we laugh at ourselves in the situation, will clear our minds.

My friend Spencer Thornton and I talk about the changes that laughter brings. A laughter frenzy will clear our minds when they're bogged down in worry. And it increases our endorphin level. We need to just let go and really laugh our worries off. Spencer, an ophthalmologist, has also been an actor/performer. He helps me try to "do a laugh" in the mornings. He goes through this laughing routine, making himself go "Ha, ha, ha, ha, ha!" to get his body tuned for laughing.

And Spencer should know about laughter. He and his wife have both had to fight severe problems with cancer. He has shown me that laughter changes the way we focus on our presence in the world.

Someone may think this kind of laughter is a false laughter. But it's really therapeutic laughter. It's wonderful to start the day thinking about laughing and how important it is to laugh—and to laugh often! Laughter can permeate our souls so we're no longer dark and negative people. When we laugh, we perceive ourselves differently and we're radiant and bright. This internal joy shows in our actions and behavior.

Monkeys get serious when they itch. We wonder why they don't laugh, why they don't have joy. There is a part of laughter that comes from joy and happiness. It's so important that we have the true joy of God within our hearts and that it's expressed in laughter. We must laugh with joy in His presence. Because if we don't have joy, we aren't expressing true Christianity and we're turning away many people.

DISCUSSION QUESTIONS

1. What does *faith* mean to you? How do you see faith at work in your daily life?

_____

_____

_____

2. What does *grace* mean to you? List some ways you feel God's grace.

_____

_____

_____

3. What does *thanksgiving* mean to you? When do
    you feel most thankful? Least thankful? List five
    ways you can be more thankful. Practice at least
    one way every day this week.

_____

_____

_____

4. Try having a good laugh first thing in the morning.
    Does it change your outlook on the day?

_____

_____

_____

For further reflection:

*For it is by grace you have been saved, through faith—and
this not from yourselves, it is the gift of God—not by works,
so that no one can boast.*

—EPHESIANS 2:8–9

Faith and grace work together to bring us thanksgiving in the
Lord. How do these three work in your life? Describe some ways
you can focus on them to change they way you lead your life.

CHAPTER 7

THE BIRTH OF THE KINGDOM OF GOD

People will do anything to preserve life. Think about all the advertisements on television, in magazines and in newspapers for ways to live longer and look younger. Yet there's only one way to eternal life—the life we all seek—and that's found in the person of Jesus Christ.

Life truly begins when we surrender to Christ at Calvary, where He gave His life for you and me. At that moment, we're no longer preserving our current lives; we're transformed into new beings through Christ. The forgiveness of sins, the grace of God, and the hope of eternity all become ours at that moment of surrender. We admit that we've been independent and rebellious. And we ask forgiveness for being selfish and self-centered. We say, "Lord, I'm sorry for being so willful. I'm ready to be focused on you now. I'm ready to let you work through me. Amen." In a state of repentance, we hand over the reins of our life to His will and direction.

At the Alamo, Col. William B. Travis asked men to cross the line to give themselves in defending the provisional government in San Antonio as it sought Texas's independence from Mexico. That call came at great personal cost. All 200 defenders died at the Alamo.[11]

Christ asks all of us to cross the line—to give ourselves to Him. He asks us to put aside our own agendas and desires, and to submit to Him. We must not **do**, we must **surrender**.

The Alamo was a turning point in American history. Each of us faces a personal turning point when we respond to Christ. He will ask. We must answer. He tells us we will face this choice:

> *No one can serve two masters. Either he will hate the one and love the other, or he will be devoted to the one and despise the other. You cannot serve both God and Money.*
> —MATTHEW 6:24

Jesus says we must decide whom we are going to serve. He demands that we make a choice. Do we say yes to Jesus Christ, who loves us and gave Himself on the cross for us? It's not a decision to be taken lightly. Saying yes means total commitment—that we love Him with our hearts and minds and souls and strength, and that we act out that love every day in faith and thanksgiving. Paul describes our commitment this way:

> *Therefore, I urge you, brothers, in view of God's mercy, to offer your bodies as living sacrifices, holy and pleasing to God—this is your spiritual act of worship. Do not conform any longer to the pattern of this world, but be transformed by the renewing of your mind.*
> —ROMANS 12:1–2

Christianity is nothing but the person of Jesus—His miracle of birth, His life, His death to take care of our sins, and His amazing resurrection that gives us eternal life and fellowship with Him. In the person of Christ all things are centered and all things evolve. All He asks of us is to change our focus. He asks us to repent of our selfishness and worldly desires and to be willing to let Him transform us.

When we say yes to the person of Jesus Christ, completely and without reservation, the eternal kingdom of God is born in us. We are His children. We are cleansed and refreshed by Him, beginning now and lasting through eternity.

As children in the kingdom of God, our attitude can no longer be that of the world, but of God. We begin to see life differently. We no longer seek satisfaction and fulfillment in the things of this world. We have our full measure of satisfaction now and forever in God, through the person of Jesus Christ. We have the eternal view that we talked about earlier.

Surrendering to God separates us from much of the thinking of the world. We have a brand new outlook, a brand new life, an eternal faith in our eternal Father.

We no longer have faith in the world, which is based on the immediate, the seen, the now. Instead, we have faith in God—eternal faith, based on the promise of Christ and our Father to provide for us now and forever. It is not faith based on a weak human emotion. It is faith focused on God's power, love and grace.

This life goes by very quickly. Many who are in their 40s think the past twenty years have sped by. Those in their 60s think the past twenty years have gone even faster. With God's perspective, we see this time as preamble to eternity. We're cared for now and we're cared for forever.

We see God as our Father and provider, our *Jehovah-Jireh*. As a father, I have wanted very much to provide for my children. I really haven't cared much for my own circumstances and possessions, but I have always wanted to make sure my children were taken care of. And now that I'm a grandfather, I feel that desire even more. This is the same way the Lord looks at us. He wants to make sure we're provided for. And because He's God,

He can meet all our needs—now and for eternity.

As His children, we can say, "Lord, let us find our place with you for eternity and let that take away all the anxieties." Knowing and believing in eternal life in Jesus Christ gives us hope and freedom in this world.

> *It is for freedom that Christ has set us free. Stand firm, then, and do not let yourselves be burdened again by a yoke of slavery.*
>
> —GALATIANS 5:1

All of us worry about one thing or another. Until we surrender to Him, our own efforts at squashing fear and worry will fail. But when we surrender to God, we refuse to surrender to worry and the slavery it creates. His grace frees us from fear. He has taken responsibility for looking out for us. No matter how difficult life might seem today, we are in His kingdom forever. We have died to self; we live in the kingdom of God.

> *Therefore, since we are receiving a kingdom that cannot be shaken, let us be thankful.*
>
> —HEBREWS 12:28

God's kingdom is eternal and everlasting. Our thanksgiving for His future grace destroys worry! He will help us in our daily commitment of thanksgiving and surrender. He will provide the support we need in tough times. He will be our constant companion. God, the author of the universe, promises He will abide with us in this process of surrender and transformation.

> *I can do everything through him who gives me strength.*
>
> —PHILIPPIANS 4:13

Our own strength is never sufficient. Our feeble, fallible human efforts will fail, and we will fall victim to all forms of selfishness and worry—anxiety and fear, pride and control. Only through Christ can we be transformed to live a life of surrender.

We must be completely honest with ourselves and realize Christ is all; we are nothing.

> *Unless the LORD builds the house, its builders labor in vain.*
> —PSALM 127:1

We must look to Christ. None of us can do it alone. Jesus will perfect us; He will mature us; He will transform us. He will continue to work in our lives until we see Him face to face.

> *Being confident of this, that he who began a good work in you will carry it on to completion until the day of Christ Jesus.*
> —PHILIPPIANS 1:6

God has begun a work in us, and He will see it through. We need to be able to say: "God, I thank you that you began a good work in me. I thank you that, no matter how unfinished I am at the moment, you will gloriously complete your work on the day of Christ Jesus. Help me to cooperate with you as you mold me into the likeness of Jesus. Amen."

We can do all things because we have the spiritual strength of knowing that God's sovereign power has control over all eternity. We have no worries. We have no fears. Instead, we have His peace and His power, enabling us in all areas of life.

True peace is not passive; it's an active, equipping power to do the work of God. Transformation is not just an internal process. It also demands an external response. In the next chapter, let's look at how we can live that courageous life of faith, thanksgiving and grace.

DISCUSSION QUESTIONS

1. Have you crossed the line to commit your life to Jesus? If not, are you willing to do so now?

_____

_____

_____

2. List some ways Jesus has changed you since you surrendered yourself to Him.

_____

_____

_____

3. How do you feel Christ's presence in your life? How do you feel Him transforming you now? Keep a journal this week recording the ways you feel His presence.

_____

_____

_____

4. What steps do you need to take to fully rest, without fear, in the hands of Jesus?

_____

_____

_____

For further reflection:

For God so loved the world that he gave his one and only Son, that whoever believes in him shall not perish but have eternal life.

—JOHN 3:16

When we surrender ourselves to Christ, we are given eternal life through Him. Discuss how you feel His eternity in your life.

CHAPTER 8

COURAGEOUS FAITH

Being reckless causes worry. Reckless investors worry. Reckless fantasies and reckless sexuality cause worry. Therefore it's vital to be careful. Actually, being a Christian is the most conservative and safe lifestyle we can live. If we love God and don't worry, we adopt the safest form of life possible.

Conversely, one must be a little reckless in order to do well. When instructors teach skiing, they say, "You have to be a bit of a fool to be a good skier." When the instructor says to be a little foolish, he's not telling us to go and break a leg (as I've done). He's telling us to relax and not worry too much. Otherwise we can't get the truly great feeling of skiing.

In other words, we can't be overly anxious. We have to free ourselves from worries about every little concern. We have to be a little bit of a fool. A person who is free of the obsessions of worry is able to do a good job—and enjoys every area of life.

When we're totally relaxed in skiing, we can do something called "anticipation," which is just dropping down on the lower ski and letting the rebound phenomenon carry us around into a turn. It is almost effortless to do mid-turns as we get the motion down. The more we relax, the more effortless skiing becomes.

This is true in daily life as well. Worry keeps us from being courageous in our families and friendships and in our service to God. If we will just relax and come back to the basics of a simpler life, the normal routine will take care of us. In the spiritual life, if we go back to the basics of faith and trust, life becomes easy, as skiing becomes easy.

We learn to drop down in anticipation in a ski maneuver that makes skiing effortless. In life, we drop down on our knees in prayer and commit our lives to Christ, turning everything over to Him. Then, when we stand up, the run (either on the ski slope or in life) is smoother. There's very little effort. No pushing, shoving or twisting. Both allow us to perform our runs in a smoother, easier, more tranquil way, with less energy, less worry, less effort.

When we can do with less, and material things really aren't important to us, we demonstrate our faith in *Jehovah-Jireh*, the God who provides.

> *Be strong and courageous. Do not be afraid or terrified because of them, for the* LORD *your God goes with you; he will never leave you nor forsake you.*
> —DEUTERONOMY 31:6

Faith says we don't have to focus on ourselves and on our possessions. Faith says we don't need to acquire an abundance. Faith says we don't have to own more than other people. Faith says we are filled with God's presence and that is sufficient for us. Out of that faith comes the ability to love, because faith works through love and love works through faith. Then we are as a flowing river, a wellspring of life. What's inside us—the joy that's in the Lord— manifests itself as a smooth, even flow of love out of us.

GIVING COURAGEOUSLY

When we are generous, we are actually waging spiritual warfare.

What we really are doing is fighting with mammon and laughing in the face of mammon. When we give away money and possessions that other people would hoard, we are simply saying God is our supplier and we can give away what we need to give away.

Jesus teaches us about giving generously and offering hospitality when He feeds 5,000 from five loaves of bread and two fish. (See Luke 9:10-17.) As was true so many times during His ministry on earth, a crowd had gathered around Jesus. After a while, the people got hungry. The disciples weren't sure what to do, but Jesus had a plan to demonstrate His generous spirit: "You give them something to eat," He said (Luke 9:13). All the disciples could find was the fish and bread; with that food, Jesus fed a multitude. The message is clear: Do what you can with what you have, and He will provide more. Jesus teaches that we must look to heaven to get our fill of physical as well as spiritual food.

> *I have seen a grievous evil under the sun: wealth hoarded to the harm of its owner, or wealth lost through some misfortune, so that when he has a son there is nothing left for him.*
> —Ecclesiastes 5:13–14

If we worry about keeping our money and our possessions, they will do us no good, and we can't use them to benefit others. On the other hand, I know many people who give more than they earn many years, drawing from reserves. We must be givers whose inward being is thankful for what we have and who want to share with others.

Many people come to us wanting funds. It's important for us to give from our hearts. We are good stewards when we give with the joy of the Lord in our hearts. We can't give solely out of a sense of duty or out of guilt. We can't give if it only makes us feel proud of ourselves or builds us up. We can genuinely give only when we feel that God has anointed it.

It's also important to evaluate where to give our money. Just as we are good stewards in giving, we must make sure our gifts go to those who are good stewards. We should give to those organizations and individuals where the money will be most efficiently used for the Lord's work, to the greatest benefit, both now and throughout the ensuing years. As we decide where to give our money, we must try to ascertain that Jesus Christ is the center of any ministry we consider. Money should be given with a great deal of discernment and prayer in focusing on the person of Jesus Christ.

Our uneasiness about giving money goes away when we have faith that God will be our provider and we're thankful for all He has given us. Our uneasiness about how those gifts will be used goes away when we listen to the Holy Spirit about where and when to give. When we can give without anxiety, we exhibit the grace of God within our lives, and others will see the difference that God's love makes in us.

LOVING COURAGEOUSLY

There's a three-letter "S" word that everybody knows: *sex*. There's a six-letter "S" word that few people know, and very few understand: *storge*. C. S. Lewis describes it in his book *The Four Loves*.[12]

Now, there are many kinds of love. Lewis wrote about four. *Philos* is the love among friends. *Eros* is the love between man and woman. *Agape* is the love God has for us and the love we have for Him. The love experience with our friends and family helps us to understand the love of God.

The fourth love is the "S" word: *storge*, which is affection. It's like glue, holding all the other loves together This affection is the humblest love, a love without airs. It binds us together. When it enters into the other loves, it is the very medium by which they operate from day to day.

Storge plugs into our thanksgiving. As Lewis discusses *storge*, he also seems to describe it as "appreciation."[13] We can't have a constant attitude of thanksgiving without affection and appreciation. We appreciate the Lord for everything He does for us, and so we live in thanks for Him. And that thanksgiving leads to a real, intrinsic love relationship with God, which is our internal response to our surrender to Him.

All the other forms of love create the framework in which *agape* can be expressed. Those loves weave together to create a symphony of life leading to eternity.

> *And so we know and rely on the love God has for us. God is love. Whoever lives in love lives in God, and God in him.*
> —1 JOHN 4:16

We have an intimate relationship with God. This is not a mental relationship in which we may know and respect Christ. It goes deeper than that. We are actually in love with Christ! And we maturely live our faith and love.

Storge also affects the way we live out our love for others. It shouldn't be misunderstood as being the other loves; we simply respect, care for and encourage others through *storge*. It transforms our relationships with others. No longer are we worried about what we can do for ourselves. In love, we are focused on what we can do for others. At St. Luke's Cataract and Laser Institute, our job is to encourage our patients and their family members. In society, in all our relationships, we must show respect, we must encourage and we must care for one another.

Appreciation makes life meaningful because it makes meaningful relationships. No longer are we selfish. We genuinely care for others first. That includes serving others, appreciating others and encouraging others. It also includes relieving other's anxieties. When we take on their concerns and fears and worries, we do two things. First, we help them share their burdens and decrease their fears. Second, we take the focus off ourselves and put it on others in a Christlike fashion. We are living examples of *storge*.

This sincerity of appreciation constitutes the importance of relationships. We must build up relationships with others because those relationships are one of life's most beautiful blessings. The hectic pace of life can pull us back to a worldly view. We need relationships with others built on God's love to keep us focused on loving Him and seeking His will. The lack of appreciation leads us back to selfishness, which leads us back to worry. But God's Word tells us that love, integrated with *storge*, gives us peace.

Perfect love drives out fear.

—1 JOHN 4:18

Love is always sacrificial. Our *agape* love for God, as well as our love for friends and family, is realistic, sacrificial, purposeful, willing and absolute. As God guides us in love, we guide each other. Our response to God's love is to love others, respecting them, offering consistent appreciation for what they do and helping them to grow in love. We should all seek relationships of mutual encouragement.

SERVING COURAGEOUSLY

For even the Son of Man did not come to be served, but to serve, and to give his life as a ransom for many.

—MARK 10:45

One of the greatest roles in life is to be a caregiver and a servant. This embodies *storge*. Many physicians I've talked with can't wait to retire. I never want to quit! I want to be a caregiver for the rest of my life. I see many nurses who feel as I do, as well as many other people who, regardless of their current occupation, just want to be a servant to others for the rest of their lives.

Jesus is the role model for service. He is the perfect servant, the perfect caregiver. At home I have a statue of Him washing the feet of His disciples. It helps me remember His service and shows me how I can follow in His steps.

In our relationships we must remember to give, not to take. Being a caregiver keeps us from selfishness, and the worries and fears that result. Giving to others makes us stronger and makes our relationships with others stronger.

We are never happy if we desire to be served and lifted up and pampered. We're worried about how others can take care of us and meet our needs. We're selfish and that always leads to worry and anxiety. I had an aunt who stayed in bed until 10:00 A.M. every day. She always wanted to be pampered. She always wanted more, and she was never satisfied. She had the nicest husband in the world; he gave her everything. But I don't think she ever appreciated him. She just ended up dissipating and dying without ever finding satisfaction and the beautiful feeling of enjoying a life of work and service.

On the other hand, there's the story of a couple who disagree about their coffee and resolve the disagreement with love and care. The husband likes regular coffee. The wife likes flavored coffee. In their marriage, when the husband wakes first, he makes flavored coffee. When the wife wakes first, she makes regular coffee. Simple gestures of love and caregiving have a great effect on our relationships.

When I see patients, I thank them for letting me be their caregiver. This lets them know that I care for them. I don't want to be just their physician; I want to be their caregiver. I want to be a servant to them. Each of us should strive to be thankful servants in our lives. There is no greater reward from work than thankful service and caregiving.

Several of us at St. Luke's Cataract and Laser Institute have committed ourselves to recite the 13th Chapter of 1 Corinthians each day. We want to bring out what is so easy to miss in our daily lives—loving the Lord and loving others. The following is a paraphrase of this chapter, substituting words related to "caregiving" for "love" and adding some thoughts—

showing love as it meets the road of reality:

> *If I speak in the tongues of men and of angels, but have not a caregiver's heart, I am only a resounding gong or a clanging cymbal.* Therefore, if I talk about things that are important in medicine, theology and science, but really don't care for people, I'm pretty hollow.

> *If I have the gift of prophecy and can fathom all mysteries and all knowledge, and if I have a faith that can move mountains, but have not a caregiver's heart, I am nothing.* In other words, I can be smart and biblical, having the Judeo-Christian faith, but if I don't have a caregiver's heart, I'm nothing.

> *If I give all I possess to the poor and surrender my body to the flames, but am not a caregiver, I gain nothing.* I can be generous to others and tithe regularly, but unless my heart is full of godly love, and I am caring for others, I've missed what Jesus Christ came for—mainly for me to focus on Him and, as a result, be a caregiver.

> *Caregiving is patient* (How I wish I were more patient!), *caregiving is kind. Caregiving does not envy other people's caregiving or anything else.* Envy and covetousness destroy our relationship with God. He is most satisfied with us when we are most satisfied with Him. *Caregiving does not boast of caregiving or anything else.* Whatever comes, comes . . . and is taken as a matter of fact. Caregivers care because they love Jesus. *Caregiving is not proud.* Caregiving is humble. The true caregiver doesn't give care for recognition, but cares because his heart has been changed toward Christ, and he delights in the feeling of caregiving.

> *Caregiving is not rude.* It does not interrupt. *Caregiving is not self-seeking.* It is not done for the benefits the caregiver receives. *A caregiver is not easily angered. A caregiver keeps no record of wrongs.* The caregiver keeps focused on God's grace, His love, His person—and as

a result, becomes a caregiver.

A caregiver does not delight in evil but rejoices with the truth, which is God's love, His life, His light and His Son.

Caregiving always protects, always trusts. A caregiver always looks at the best in others and can be depended upon. *A caregiver always hopes* for the best *and always perseveres in the caregiving.* For example, the Good Samaritan (see Luke 10:25–37) gave time and money while he was of poor background. Yet he was greater than the priest or the lawyer, who were interested in their position and did not care.

Caregiving never fails. But where there are prophecies and wisdoms, *they will cease; where there are tongues* and great orations and talks, *they will be stilled; where there is* great medical and theological *knowledge, it will pass away quickly.*

For we know in part, we know a little bit about what is involved in caring for patients and others, and we guess what may come in the future, *but when perfection comes,* when Christ comes, *the imperfect disappears.*

When I was a child, throughout my pilgrimage on earth learning to be a better caregiver, *I talked like a child, I thought like a child, I reasoned like a child. When I became a man,* when I became truly mature, *I put childish ways behind me* (though those closest to me may not see it sometimes).

Now we see but a poor reflection as in a mirror of the things that are going to come; *then we shall see* the Lord *face to face. Now I know in part* about God and theology from the Bible and the Holy Spirit; *then I shall know fully,* and that is full intimacy, *even as I am fully known.* As a Christian, I seek God's intimacy more than anything. I need God's intimacy to be a caregiver.

And now these three remain: faith, hope, and caregiving.

But the greatest of these is caregiving. It changes us first
on the inside and then on the outside. Faith works
through love, and hope results from it. Caregiving is the
love we show to others in our families, in our social relationships and in our profession of medicine.

May each of us follow the way of caregiving and eagerly
desire spiritual gifts—especially the gift of godly wisdom.

Caregiving is the ultimate expression of love, appreciation
and encouragement. It's the greatest result of *storge* mixing with
the other loves of our lives, changing our focus and our attitudes, taking us from selfishness to sacrifice. When we serve
others in genuine love and care, we don't have time to worry.
When we focus on the needs of others, our own needs and
desires fade away. We don't have the energy to focus on ourselves. And we are filled with the joy of serving God's people as
He directed us to do.

As we learn to trust in God's future grace, we are transformed
inside and out. This transformation enables us to see God as
He truly is—our constant provider, our agent of change, our
Lord and Redeemer and Friend. Amen.

DISCUSSION QUESTIONS

1. List some ways you can live a life of courageous
    faith this week.

    _____

    _____

    _____

2. What keeps you from giving courageously?

    _____

    _____

    _____

3. Apply *storge* to your relationships with others. How does it change them?

_____

_____

_____

4. Do you know caregivers? Ask them why they serve others.

_____

_____

_____

For further reflection:

Give, and it will be given to you. A good measure, pressed down, shaken together and running over, will be poured into your lap. For with the measure you use, it will be measured to you.

—LUKE 6:38

We must have an attitude of giving. When we give, we make our life doubly meaningful. What are some ways you can give and serve?

CHAPTER 9

GROWING IN GOD

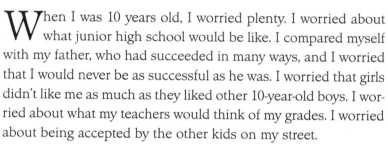

When I was 10 years old, I worried plenty. I worried about what junior high school would be like. I compared myself with my father, who had succeeded in many ways, and I worried that I would never be as successful as he was. I worried that girls didn't like me as much as they liked other 10-year-old boys. I worried about what my teachers would think of my grades. I worried about being accepted by the other kids on my street.

At age 20, I worried about how I would do in college, about what kind of athlete I would be, about whether I would be accepted by others—especially girls. And while I was leading my youth group in college, I was not the model Christian on the weekends. I struggled with my priorities and with balancing the lures of the world and being centered in Christ.

When I was 30, I was married, finishing my medical residency and starting as a professor at Duke University. I was worried about my career—what kind of papers to present and publish, how to be accepted in academic and professional circles. And I was worried about my marriage. Ours wasn't perfect. Both of us tried to see what we could get, rather than what Christ could give.

By age 40, I was worrying about my medical practice—caring for patients, finding my way through the professional politics and my lack of acceptance, even though I had greatly succeeded. What were my kids going to do? What about my wife? Was our marriage going to last?

At 50, I was more concerned about holding on. The demands of work were so great that I didn't have much time for anything but to go home, rest and work out so I could stay fit to work, read the Scripture and pray. Life became a whole lot of just focusing on work and trying to have joy in work.

On my 60th birthday I looked back and was amazed at how much I had struggled with worry through the years. But I also think I learned a lot about dealing with worry. I've learned it isn't important whether I work harder or work less. It's more important for me to have enough faith in God's eternal grace so His peace and joy and contentment can blossom forth. And I've learned to be thankful that I'm alive and enjoy my work, that my children have done well, and that I have beautiful grandchildren. I'm thankful life has worked out as well as it has.

When I'm 70 and, God willing, 80, I think it will continue to be the same as it's been since I was 10. I'll still be worried about being accepted by others and being successful. I'll worry about my marriage and about my children and grandchildren. I'll still struggle with worry and practice being continually thankful.

Complete faith and trust hasn't happened for me overnight. I wasn't permanently rid of worry when one day I said, "Lord, I'll let you do everything." It's been cycles of more trust and less trust, more thanksgiving and less thanksgiving, more surrender and less surrender. It's been a process of making many, many mistakes and spending a lot of time on my knees listening to and talking with God. And I still have room to grow.

When each of us crosses the line and commits our life to the person of Jesus Christ, we're plunged into a process of transformation. We don't always make clear progress. Sometimes it's two steps forward and three back. Now we hope that the three steps back are small and that there are more steps forward overall. But we must go through all the steps as we grow in our intimacy with Christ.

We should never waver in our commitment to His process of transformation. Few things are accomplished immediately. No one can decide one day he will run a marathon the next. He must train diligently for months.

It's the same way with our spiritual transformation. We cannot be transformed in a day. But we commit to the process every day.

Life is much like the eighth round of a ten-round fight. We have to keep getting up and getting back in the ring. We might have taken hits in the past; we might have even been knocked down by events. But we need to get up every morning determined to keep going. And we need to let that persistence extend throughout the day, every day. We have to keep our focus on God, despite all the attacks we face from the world.

All of us have times in our lives when we feel up and times when we feel down. But we can't let our inner peace be destroyed by outside circumstances and events. In those down times, we still need to be filled with thanksgiving.

> I will extol the LORD at all times; his praise will always be on my lips.
>
> —PSALM 34:1

Our praise and thanksgiving will keep us strong in the up and down cycles we face as we are transformed. We're all going through this process of transformation—of focusing on God and not on ourselves. The struggle against selfishness and worry is a continual one; and one that should be continued. When we accept His call to be His children, we commit ourselves to building an intimate, personal relationship with the person of Jesus Christ.

This relationship is not perfected until we join Him in heaven. We should never say we've attained complete transformation on earth. Our salvation doesn't make us perfect, but it does change our focus. We're still full of the world and its lies and agendas. The cares and deceits of this world can easily creep in on all of us. I'm not perfect. As the license plate says, "I'm just getting better through Christ." I'm just a sinner who is in the state of repentance, struggling to take my focus away from the world and place it on God. It's a constant process of focusing and refocusing. Praise God, for His grace brings us back to Him with love and kindness.

I also have a secret weapon. I know I already have ultimate victory because I believe in God and His future grace. Jesus assures us of this victory.

> *I have told you these things, so that in me you may have peace. In this world you will have trouble. But take heart! I have overcome the world.*
>
> —JOHN 16:33

The world can throw all it wants at us; we have the ultimate partner in our corner. We have an intimate, personal relationship with the King of kings and the Lord of lords. We have victory over the world through Jesus Christ!

So why do we struggle with being thankful? Why can't we conquer worry? We're easily diverted from our focus on God because we look for satisfaction in other areas. We let our minds get cluttered with worldly attitudes and perspectives rather than the eternal perspective and values of God.

There's no question that the greatest fulfillment and peace is in the unseen and the eternal. Yet it's very difficult to sustain deep faith and trust. So often we sacrifice the unseen and the eternal for the very temporary and relatively worthless present time. Maintaining deep faith violates our normal, human way of thinking—of wanting to be independent and self-sufficient, desiring to take care of ourselves. Faith in God is faith in the supernatural—God's power beyond the natural world. This is not a mental trick or gimmick. We may not understand it because it's mystical. But we know, full of faith, that He helps us because He knows us. After all, He's the one who made us.

> For you created my inmost being;
>   you knit me together in my mother's womb.
> I praise you because I am fearfully and wonderfully
> made; your works are wonderful,
>   I know that full well.
> My frame was not hidden from you
>   when I was made in the secret place.
> When I was woven together in the depths of the earth,
>   your eyes saw my unformed body.
> All the days ordained for me
>   were written in your book before one of them came to
>   be.
>
> —Psalm 139:13–16

Remember, God created us. He didn't just create the world and set it in motion, then walk away. He was intimately involved in the creation of each of us. He has unsurpassed knowledge of us. And He is intimately involved in our transformation. Philippians 1:6 says he "began a good work" in us. He has started the process. He will see it through to completion.

In Hebrew 12:1, Paul compares this process with running a race. "Let us run with perseverance the race marked out for us." As a long-distance runner, I know the conditioning that's required for races. I used to run 23 miles every other day to prepare for 100-mile races. I used special instruments to condition me for higher altitudes. I ate various types of food and wore the lightest clothes for the climate. I carried special clothes in case it rained or got windy while I was training. And as race day got closer, I studied the map and plotted my course carefully.

The conditioning paid off. In one 100-mile race, I was one of only three competitors to finish. Some of the runners quit because of the snow and the cold. Others got lost. But we were prepared. Not only were we committed with our minds and our bodies, we also were committed with our hearts. We wanted to run the race and so we prepared for it.

God wants us to be prepared for the conditions the world throws at us. He wants us to be ready for the times when we face the hardships, worries or desires of the world. Because He created us, He knows how we function best.

He knows what will help us and what will hurt us. He is our partner, coach and guide. When we seek Him, He will reveal His plans and His vision. With our minds, hearts and bodies we must commit to Him. The training regimen consists of the Three F's: being faithful, fervent and focused.

FAITHFUL

Being faithful means having the basic truth of Christ; having faith not in ourselves, but in God. Faith is the essence of all our strength in God. Faith is in what we *know*. We *know* we have a Creator, and by the Word of God we *know* we have a Redeemer. We are satisfied with all that God is for us in Jesus. In faith we strive to know Him in spirit and in our actions. We seek to take on the mind of Christ, rather than hold onto our rebellious worldly minds.

> *I want to know Christ and the power of his resurrection.*
> —PHILIPPIANS 3:10

In this passage in Philippians, Paul talks about "knowing" on an intimate level. For example, in a marriage the partners "know" each other through physical, emotional and intellectual intimacy.

In that same sort of "marriage" relationship with Jesus Christ, everything is found in Him and our total life is committed to Him. We are with Him in our waking and our sleeping. Our lives are lived in prayer and petition; we look to Him and not to our-selves. In fact, our very first petition should be that we become intimate with Him so that by living in His presence we will constantly seek His guidance, His wisdom, His knowledge and His strength. We know that He is real and relevant. We know His power and direction in our lives. We know He sustains us.

Knowing Him comes by staying in God's Word—the Bible. We have to be with God in the Word and in the Holy Spirit to grow spiritually and to carry out His work.

The Word of God must be made real in us. When we let the Word of God dwell in us richly, the Spirit takes that Word and makes it part of us. It transforms our minds and it shapes our desires, our focus and our leanings.

> *But his delight is in the law of the* LORD,
>   *and on his law he meditates day and night.*
> *He is like a tree planted by streams of water,*
>   *which yields its fruit in season*
> *and whose leaf does not wither.*
>   *Whatever he does prospers.*
>
> —PSALM 1:2–3

We need to fill ourselves with the quotations of God. Meditation on the Word every day and seeking the Lord through His Word will give us a mindset of peace. Memorize Scripture. And then use that Scripture in your prayers. We can pray the Word back to the Lord, inserting our names. And then we can plant our feet firmly on earth and stand on those claims that are written about us as His children.

> *You will keep in perfect peace him whose mind is steadfast,*
> *because he trusts in you.*
>
> —ISAIAH 26:3

In this verse, Isaiah was implying that he had peace when he read God's Word and trusted in it, rather than trusting in his own intelligence. This was no small feat. Isaiah may have been one of the most intelligent men of the Old Testament. It took a great deal of effort, will and commitment for him to trust God first, rather than his own intellect. Isaiah's faithfulness was essential to his transformation.

If we are to have perfect peace, our minds must be fixed on God and His kingdom and not on the world. Devoting time every day to reading the Bible helps us fight worry. And one of the best ways to get the Word of God into every part of our lives is to try to memorize verses.

> *My son, pay attention to what I say;*
> *listen closely to my words.*
> *Do not let them out of your sight,*
> *keep them within your heart;*
> *for they are life to those who find them*
> *and health to a man's whole body.*
>
> —PROVERBS 4:20–22

We are the soil and we have to be ready for the Word. May every word be sown into us so that it gives a hundred-fold return, and not a thousand words that give no return. Often I have merely read many words without perceiving or receiving their meaning and truth. Conversely, I can meditate for days and days, for years and years, on one word. We must truly meditate on the Word and have that Word dictate the thoughts of our hearts.

> *Do not let this Book of the Law depart from your mouth;*
> *meditate on it day and night, so that you may be careful to*
> *do everything written in it. Then you will be prosperous and*
> *successful.*
>
> —JOSHUA 1:8

Here God tells Joshua that if he follows the directions God has written and if he is rooted in the Scripture, then God will provide. We must be the same way. Each day we must proclaim the Word of God, the truth of God. We must pray it, we must say it, we must believe it and we must live it. That is the only way to be faithful.

FERVENT

Faith builds on our passion, desire and inner longing for intimacy with God. We must have the desire to be focused and aligned to Christ in a way that truly makes us want to be healed from all the evils of the world. That desire includes healing from worry and living in a thanksgiving frenzy. It's a passionate cry of focusing on the Lord.

> *As the deer pants for streams of water,*
> *so my soul pants for you, O God.*
> *My soul thirsts for God, for the living God.*
> —PSALM 42:1–2

We surrender to God not out of duty, but out of love. We love Him; we embrace Him with our whole being. And we seek His presence in our lives. We seek an intimate relationship with Him. God saves us through His grace to make us like Jesus Christ, and He wants us to desire what He wants.

So the path of transformation must include desire. We must desire to be transformed; we must desire to be more Christlike. We can't just know in our heads who Christ is and how to be like Him. We must have the desire in our hearts. That desire transforms us. We love God and are in love with Him! We're overwhelmed with thanksgiving and joy because our hearts are filled with love for the person of Jesus Christ.

> *Sing and make music in your heart to the Lord, always giving thanks to God the Father for everything, in the name of our Lord Jesus Christ.*
> —EPHESIANS 5:19–20

If all we desire are the things of this world, we'll fail. We will fall victim to selfishness, to our independent spirits. But our passion for the living God will keep us close to Him. When love is present in a marriage, it's much easier to keep the relationship

on track. When we find love in our relationship with God, growing close to Him is easier. We're lifted off this earth and freed
from the cares of this world. We're engulfed in His presence and
stand fast in His promises.

FOCUSED

A cousin of mine went through medical school. He was very
bright and was successful in school. He once told me, though,
that the secret to medical school was not intelligence. It was dili-
gence. "You know, the difference between those who made it
and those who didn't is sticking with it. Those who failed were
quitters. They weren't dedicated enough to keep on going."

That persistence is what helps us succeed in everything. To
be transformed, to become Christlike, we must be focused on
Him. We must refuse to be distracted. We must never look back,
or to the left or to the right. We must look only at Christ.

Now Satan would love to work on us and get us off the path.
He would love for us to start feeling proud of how well we're
doing in our relationships with God. He would love for us to
think we have enough passion and faith to get through. He
would love for us to think it's OK for us to stay where we are,
that we don't need to grow any further. In fact, because we're
doing so well, we might think we don't need God quite as much.
Then we start slipping back into our independent natures.

We start comparing ourselves with others. We start worrying
about whether we have everything we need. We take our eyes
off God and start noticing the things of the world. Paul warns
us to guard against this attitude and tells us how to stay
focused. Let's look again at chapter 12 of Hebrews:

> Let us throw off everything that hinders and the sin that so
> easily entangles, and let us run with perseverance the race
> marked out for us. Let us fix our eyes on Jesus, the author
> and perfecter of our faith, who for the joy set before him
> endured the cross, scorning its shame, and sat down at the

right hand of the throne of God.
—HEBREWS 12:1–2

We have to be persistent—stubborn in our faith, stubborn in our desire and stubborn in our determination that nothing can shake us from our focus on God. He loves us. He is faithful in His provisions for us. Nothing can separate us from His love. There is no other way for us to respond than with that same determination, based in love, joy and thanksgiving.

None of us should ever give up. We should never say we've attained perfect transformation. But through His grace we grow closer to Him through Jesus Christ. The kingdom of God will be there as we wait for Him now, as we work for Him, as we live with Jesus in our hearts, as we see what God does through us as we go forward in faith.

> *Therefore, since we have been justified through faith, we have peace with God through our Lord Jesus Christ, through whom we have gained access by faith into this grace in which we now stand. And we rejoice in the hope of the glory of God.*
> —ROMANS 5:1–2

When we turn our total being away from worry, when we trust in God's grace and get rid of all the worldly distractions, when we live in a thanksgiving frenzy, we are wrapped up in a cloud of exuberance transcending this world. This state of transformation keeps us, so that when we are ultimately translated into God's presence in heaven we'll find our exuberance multiplied immeasurably.

DISCUSSION QUESTIONS

1. Do you worry more or worry less than you did when you were younger? Do you worry about the same things?

_____

_____

_____

2. List some ways you can practice being faithful to Christ this week.

_____

_____

_____

3. How do you feel passion for God's presence?

_____

_____

_____

4. What obstacles keep you from being focused on the Lord? Describe some ways you can overcome them this week.

_____

_____

_____

For further reflection:

Finally, brothers, whatever is true, whatever is noble, whatever is right, whatever is pure, whatever is lovely, whatever is admirable—if anything is excellent or praiseworthy—think about such things.

—PHILIPPIANS 4:8

The process of transformation continues until we are united with God in heaven. Paul tells us how to align our thoughts to our benefit and His glory while we're earthly beings. Discuss ways you can focus on the true, noble, right, pure, lovely and admirable qualities and blessings of the Lord.

CONCLUSION

A lecturer was giving a talk to about 400 students and instructors at a New England college. The lecturer asked, "How many of you look forward to a better future?" Not one person raised a hand. The audience members felt so burdened by anxiety and worry that they didn't think the future would be better. They didn't look forward with hope. Instead, they were struggling to handle the problems they faced. Their daily lives were so troubling to them, they couldn't even think about tomorrow.

Does this sound like anyone you know? I'm sure all of us, at some point in our lives, have been bogged down by problems and fears. Maybe it was a test in school, a relationship that became difficult, pressure at work, financial concerns at home or health problems. It can feel like a bottomless pit of fear and anxiety, a pit from which we think there is no escape.

Those feelings are based on our attitude about the future. If we fear the unknown, we worry. We're afraid to make decisions, and then when we're forced to make them, we tend to make bad ones. We let events and people make us negative, critical and unhappy. We're selfish and controlling. We're no fun to be around.

But when we have a relationship with God in the person of Jesus Christ, we know the future. We know that we have eternity with the author and creator of the universe. We are engulfed in His grace today and every day.

Let us prize and treasure His eternity. When we look to the

future knowing that God will take care of us, we're not directed by worry. We can make wise decisions because we base them on His will. We're not negative and critical. We're intercessors and caregivers. We're filled with the fruit of the Holy Spirit: love, joy, peace, patience, kindness, goodness, faithfulness, gentleness and self-control.

We're free from the worries of this world. We rejoice in God always. We're filled with a spirit of thanksgiving. Thanksgiving includes the *storge*, the affection, that C. S. Lewis writes about.[14] Thanksgiving includes the realization of who and what we are, and who God is—the thanks for His grace. Thanksgiving is a constant state of being thankful in all things, being thankful for the glass that's half-full rather than worried about the glass that's half-empty.

Think of the many sins involved in worry: unbelief, doubt, selfishness, covetousness and disobedience. Worry replaces God's peace with human despair. Thanksgiving is choked out by bitterness and resentment. Our noisy worry keeps us from hearing His still, small voice. We don't wait on the Lord, but we mumble against the manna He gives us. We want more and seek Him less. We doubt God's goodness, doubt His faithfulness, doubt His truthfulness, doubt His love, doubt His wisdom and doubt His eternity.

Worry reaches beyond our own lives and starts a chain reaction in those around us. We start complaining and criticizing. We're unpleasant, so others avoid us. We don't have joy in our own lives, which hinders the joy and peace in others.

But a spirit of thanksgiving takes the focus off ourselves and puts us in proper perspective. It gives us the proper position and purpose not only externally, but internally. Thanksgiving is the opposite of fear and worry.

> For you did not receive a spirit that makes you a slave again
> to fear, but you received the Spirit of sonship. And by him we
> cry "Abba, Father." The Spirit himself testifies with our spirit

that we are God's children. Now if we are children, then we are
heirs–heirs of God and co-heirs with Christ, if indeed we share
in his sufferings in order that we may also share in his glory.
—ROMANS 8:15–17

Now we can choose to live by the standards of this world and become "slaves to fear," as Paul calls it. Or we can choose a new world—a world in which we intimately know our magnificent God and experience His perfect grace. We need to be thankful forever to our God, our creator, our eternal partner in this existence. His grace comes down and overshadows all our sins. The ecstasy of thanksgiving fills us when we realize He is within us and will be with us forever.

I was at a prison ministry when a speaker asked, "Are you serving time or is time serving you?" I think this applies to all of us. All we have is time. Are we filling it with anxiety, fear and worry? Or are we filling it with thanksgiving? If we're serving time, we're just marking it; and in effect we're wasting it. We're simply enduring, wasting life by looking at it as a duty. In that mindset, we fill a lot of time with worry because we lack hope in the future.

But if time is serving us, we're using it to strengthen our relationship with God. We're bound to God through His future grace. We are confident, courageous and committed to Him.

We're using time to serve those around us through His power and love. We're caregivers who live out *storge* in our daily lives, supporting and appreciating others. A spirit of thanksgiving connects us to the real source of power and strength: the eternal God.

The mental attitude we must have to use time properly is an attitude of thanksgiving unto God, a thankful spirit. Let us look at the minutes and be thankful for them. We need to treasure each moment, at work and at home with our loved ones. Treasuring the present allows the peace and joy of the Lord to fill us.

Peace I leave with you; my peace I give you. I do not give to

you as the world gives. Do not let your hearts be troubled
and do not be afraid.

—JOHN 14:27

The peace of God is different from the false peace of the world. We rest all of our hopes on the person of Jesus Christ, who has given Himself for us. In thanksgiving, we clear our minds of the desires and agendas of the world and align ourselves with Him. He gives us eternal grace when we're engulfed with Him. He will be our appreciation, our *storge*, our desire and our thanksgiving, now and forever.

My mouth will speak in praise of the LORD.
Let every creature praise his holy name for ever and ever.

—PSALM 145:21

During long races, I quote scriptures and go into a thanksgiving frenzy. For twenty-four to thirty hours of racing, I don't think of myself. I don't think about the race or the physical effort or let my thoughts make me tired. Instead, I focus with thanksgiving on God. I think upward. I look to Him. In the race of life, we need to think about God. We need to be full of thanksgiving for His grace and presence.

A thankful heart unto a sovereign God gets rid of our worry. Not just thanksgiving for our material blessings, because that may be considered self-centered; but thankfulness for God Himself which lets us be engulfed in His presence now and for eternity. Thanksgiving destroys the worried heart and leads to the peaceful heart.

God's peace is essential in the fight against worry. Sometimes we convince ourselves that we're not worried when we really are. The test is whether we have God's peace—the peace that passes all understanding.

This peaceful heart is the foundation for joy. We have peace with a fountain of joy springing forth when we are thankful for the sovereignty of God—the Fatherhood that will provide for our entire existence through all eternity.

Thanksgiving and joy change us. Our relationships with family and friends are stronger and deeper. Our work becomes more meaningful. Thanksgiving enables us to know God. There is no better way to engage Him than by living in a thanksgiving frenzy for Him: We love Him, we worship Him, we adore Him. We enter into His Presence and are engulfed by Him. We're in His hands forever. We rest in His peace. We trust in God's eternal plan.

> *"For I know the plans I have for you,"* declares the LORD, *"plans to prosper you and not to harm you, plans to give you hope and a future."*
>
> —JEREMIAH 29:11

We have eternal hope and provision in the Lord. The cares of the world can no longer weigh us down. He is God! He gives us the ultimate victory over worry!

The final answer to worry is our relationship with the Lord and faith in His future grace. We must constantly thank Him and appreciate Him for His grace. Fellowship with the person of Jesus Christ is our highest goal. Great praise and thanksgiving ensure that our relationship with Him and our love for Him are magnified every day.

What keeps us from being thankful to the Lord? Anything that clutters our minds and takes our focus off God. What keeps us from being focused? Selfishness and sinfulness. We must live a life of faith in His grace. He is Lord! He is God! He is responsible for us now and for eternity. As we look to God, His peace and presence within us make us complete. We're free from worry. We radiate with joy. Thanks be to God for His grace now and forever! Amen!

PUTTING PROMISES INTO ACTION

Are you worried about a specific relationship or circumstance? This index lists some key Bible verses you can use to battle worry and fear. These verses are God's promises that He is with us and will be our support and strength. Read them. Believe them. Let His Word become the foundation in your struggles!

ARE YOU WORRIED, ANXIOUS, AFRAID OR TROUBLED?

GOD WILL GIVE YOU PEACE.

In my distress I called to the LORD;
I cried to my God for help.
From his temple he heard my voice;
my cry came before him, into his ears.
He brought me out into a spacious place;
he rescued me because he delighted in me.

—PSALM 18:6, 19

God is our refuge and strength,
    an ever-present help in trouble.
Therefore we will not fear, though the earth give way
    and the mountains fall into the heart of the sea.

—PSALM 46:1–2

When I am afraid,
    I will trust in you.
In God, whose word I praise,
    in God I trust; I will not be afraid.
What can mortal man do to me?

—PSALM 56:3–4

You will keep in perfect peace him whose mind is steadfast, because he trusts in you.

—ISAIAH 26:3

Do not let your hearts be troubled. Trust in God; trust also in me . . . Peace I leave with you; my peace I give you. I do not give to you as the world gives. Do not let your hearts be troubled and do not be afraid.

—JOHN 14:1, 27

I have told you these things, so that in me you may have peace. In this world you will have trouble. But take heart! I have overcome the world.

—JOHN 16:33

Do not be anxious about anything, but in everything, by prayer and petition, with thanksgiving, present your requests to God. And the peace of God, which transcends all understanding, will guard your hearts and your minds in Christ Jesus.

—PHILIPPIANS 4:6–7

ARE YOU WORRIED ABOUT THE FUTURE?
GOD WILL GUIDE YOU.

He guides the humble in what is right and teaches them his way.

—PSALM 25:9

I will instruct you and teach you in the way you should go; I will counsel you and watch over you.

—PSALM 32:8

If the LORD delights in a man's way,
*   he makes his steps firm;*
Though he stumble, he will not fall,
*   for the LORD upholds him with his hand.*

—PSALM 37:23–24

Trust in the LORD with all your heart and lean not on your own understanding; in all your ways acknowledge him, and he will make your paths straight.

—PROVERBS 3:5

Commit to the LORD whatever you do, and your plans will succeed.

—PROVERBS 16:3

So do not fear, for I am with you;
*   do not be dismayed, for I am your God.*
I will strengthen you and help you;
*   I will uphold you with my righteous right hand.*

—ISAIAH 41:10

"For I know the plans I have for you," declares the LORD, "plans to prosper you and not to harm you, plans to give you hope and a future."

—JEREMIAH 29:11

If any of you lacks wisdom, he should ask God, who gives generously to all without finding fault, and it will be given to him.

—JAMES 1:5

ARE YOU AFRAID OF FEELING ALONE?
GOD WILL NEVER LEAVE YOU.

Be strong and courageous. Do not be afraid or terrified because of them, for the LORD your God goes with you; he will never leave you nor forsake you.

—DEUTERONOMY 31:6

Then you will call, and the LORD will answer; you will cry for help, and he will say: Here am I.

—ISAIAH 58:9

The LORD your God is with you,
*   he is mighty to save.*
He will take great delight in you,
*   he will quiet you with his love,*
*   he will rejoice over you with singing.*

—ZEPHANIAH 3:17

I will not leave you as orphans; I will come to you.

—JOHN 14:18

ARE YOU WORRIED NO ONE LOVES YOU?
GOD LOVES YOU.

For God so loved the world that he gave his one and only Son, that whoever believes in him shall not perish but have eternal life.

—JOHN 3:16

For I am convinced that neither death nor life, neither angels nor demons, neither the present nor the future, nor any powers, neither height nor depth, nor anything else in all creation, will be able to separate us from the love of God that is in Christ Jesus our Lord.

—ROMANS 8:38–39

This is how we know what love is: Jesus Christ laid down his life for us. And we ought to lay down our lives for our brothers.

—1 JOHN 3:16

This is love: not that we loved God, but that he loved us and sent his Son as an atoning sacrifice for our sins.

—1 JOHN 4:10

ARE YOU WORRIED THAT GOD COULD NEVER FORGIVE YOUR SINS?

GOD'S SALVATION OVERCOMES ALL SINS AND GUILT.

*As far as the east is from the west,
  so far has he removed our transgressions from us.*

—PSALM 103:12

If we confess our sins, he is faithful and just and will forgive us our sins and purify us from all unrighteousness.

—1 JOHN 1:9

DO YOU FEEL DEPRESSED?

GOD WILL COMFORT YOU.

The LORD is close to the brokenhearted and saves those who are crushed in spirit.

—PSALM 34:18

Why are you downcast, O my soul?
  Why so disturbed within me?
Put your hope in God,
  for I will yet praise him,
  my Savior and my God.

—PSALM 42:11

ARE YOU WORRIED BECAUSE YOU FACE OPPOSITION?
GOD IS WITH YOU.

If God is for us, who can be against us?

—ROMANS 8:31

ARE YOU WORRIED ABOUT PHYSICAL NEEDS?
GOD WILL PROVIDE.

Therefore I tell you, do not worry about your life, what you will eat or drink; or about your body, what you will wear. Is not life more important than food, and the body more important than clothes? Look at the birds of the air; they do not sow or reap or store away in barns, and yet your heavenly Father feeds them. Are you not much more valuable than they? Who of you by worrying can add a single hour to his life?

And why do you worry about clothes? See how the lilies of the field grow. They do not labor or spin. Yet I tell you that not even Solomon in all his splendor was dressed like one of these. If that is how God clothes the grass of the field, which is here today and tomorrow is thrown into the fire, will he not much more clothe you, O you of little faith? So do not worry, saying, "What shall we eat?" or "What shall we wear?" For the pagans run after all these things, and your heavenly Father knows that you need them. But seek first his kingdom and his righteousness and all these things will be given to you as well. Therefore do not worry about tomorrow, for tomorrow will worry about itself. Each day has enough trouble of its own.

—MATTHEW 6:25–34

If you, then, though you are evil, know how to give good gifts to your children, how much more will your Father in heaven give good gifts to those who ask him!

—MATTHEW 7:11

Are not five sparrows sold for two pennies? Yet not one of them is forgotten by God. Indeed, the very hairs of your head are all numbered. Don't be afraid; you are worth more than many sparrows.

—LUKE 12:6–7

He who did not spare his own Son, but gave him up for us all—how will he not also, along with him, graciously give us all things?

—ROMANS 8:32

And God is able to make all grace bound to you, so that in all things at all times, having all that you need, you will abound in every good work.

—2 CORINTHIANS 9:8

And my God will meet all your needs according to his glorious riches in Christ Jesus.

—PHILIPPIANS 4:19

DO YOU WORRY ABOUT YOUR SAFETY?
GOD WILL PROTECT YOU.

I will lie down and sleep in peace,
for you alone, O LORD,
make me dwell in safety.

—PSALM 4:8

The LORD will keep you from all harm—
he will watch over your life;
the LORD will watch over your coming and going
both now and forevermore.

—PSALM 121:7–8

DO YOU WORRY SO MUCH
THAT YOU CAN'T SLEEP?
GOD WILL EASE YOUR FEARS.

I lie down and sleep; I wake again, because the LORD sustains me.

—PSALM 3:5

I will lie down and sleep in peace for you alone, O LORD, make me dwell in safety.

—PSALM 4:8

When you lie down, you will not be afraid;
* when you lie down, your sleep will be sweet.*

—PROVERBS 3:24

ARE YOU WORRIED ABOUT
YOUR APPEARANCE?
GOD LOOKS IN YOUR HEART.

But the LORD said to Samuel, "Do not consider his appearance or his height, for I have rejected him. The LORD does not look at the things man looks at. Man looks at the outward appearance, but the LORD looks at the heart."

—1 SAMUEL 16:7

He has made everything beautiful in its time. He has also set eternity in the hearts of men; yet they cannot fathom what God has done from beginning to end.

—ECCLESIASTES 3:11

ARE YOU WORRIED ABOUT YOUR HEALTH?
GOD WILL GIVE YOU STRENGTH.

A righteous man may have many troubles, but the LORD delivers him from them all.

—PSALM 34:19

The LORD will guide you always;
he will satisfy your needs in a sun-scorched land and
will strengthen your frame.

—ISAIAH 58:11

"But I will restore you to health and heal your wounds,"
declares the LORD, "because you are called an outcast, Zion
for whom no one cares."

—JEREMIAH 30:17

Is any one of you sick? He should call the elders of the church to pray over him and anoint him with oil in the name of the Lord. And the prayer offered in faith will make the sick person well; the Lord will raise him up.

—JAMES 5:14–15

ARE YOU WORRIED ABOUT GETTING OLD?
GOD WILL STAY WITH YOU.

The righteous will flourish like a palm tree,
they will grow like a cedar of Lebanon;
planted in the house of the LORD,
they will flourish in the courts of our God.
They will still bear fruit in old age,
they will stay fresh and green.

—PSALM 92:12–14

Even to your old age and gray hairs I am he, I am he who will sustain you.

—ISAIAH 46:4

ARE YOU WORRIED ABOUT DYING?
GOD OFFERS ETERNAL LIFE.

Even though I walk
through the valley of the shadow of death,
I will fear no evil,
for you are with me;
your rod and your staff,
they comfort me.

—PSALM 23:4

For God so loved the world that he gave his one and only Son, that whoever believes in him shall not perish but have eternal life.

—JOHN 3:16

I give them eternal life, and they shall never perish; no one can snatch them out of my hand.

—JOHN 10:28

"Where, O death, is you victory?
Where, O death, is your sting?"
Thanks be to God! He gives us the victory
through our Lord Jesus Christ.

—1 CORINTHIANS 15:55, 57

Since the children have flesh and blood, he too shared in their humanity so that by his death he might destroy him who holds the power of death—that is, the devil—and free those who all their lives were held in slavery by their fear of death.

—HEBREWS 2:14–15

NOTES

1. Charles Horace Mayo, *Aphorisms of Dr. Charles Horace Mayo*, 1865–1939, and Dr. William James Mayo, 1861–1939. (Springfield, IL: Charles C. Thomas, 1951.)

2. *The American Heritage Dictionary of the English Language*. Third edition. (Boston: Houghton Mifflin Company, 1992).

3. Martyn Lloyd-Jones, *Be Still My Soul* (Ann Arbor, MI: Servant Publications, 1995).

4. Martin Luther, *Three Treatises* (Philadelphia: Fortress Press, 1960).

5. Eberhard Bethge, *Dietrich Bonhoeffer* (NY: Harper and Row, 1970).

6. *Volcanic Eruptions of 1980 at Mount St. Helens, The First 100 Days*, U.S. Geological Survey Professional Paper 1249. (Foxworthy and Hill, 1982).

7. Spanoudis, Stephen L., *Quotations–Quotes by Women*. 1991. http://www.geocities.com/~spandoudi/quote-09c.html.

8. Ibid.

9. *Autobiography of George Mueller*. (London: J. Nisbet and Co., 1906).

10. John Piper, *Future Grace* (Sisters, OR: Multnomah Publishers, Inc., 1995).

11. McDonald, Archid P., *William Barrett [i.e. Barret] Travis, a Biography*. (Austin, TX: Eakins Press, 1976).

12. C. S. Lewis, *The Four Loves* (NY: Harcourt Brace & Company, 1960).

13. Ibid.

14. Ibid.

Scripture Index

Bibliography

Best, S. Payne. *The Venlo Incident*. London: Hutchinson, 1950.

Bethge, Eberhard. *Dietrich Bonhoeffer*. NY: Harper and Row, 1970.

Edwards, Jonathan. *The Works of Jonathan Edwards*. Edinburgh: Banner of Truth Trust, 1974, orig. 1834.

Lewis, C. S. *The Four Loves*. NY: Harcourt Brace & Company, 1960.

Lloyd-Jones, Martyn. *Be Still My Soul*. Ann Arbor, MI: Servant Publications, 1995.

Luther, Martin. *Three Treatises*. Philadelphia: Fortress Press, 1960.

Piper, John. *Future Grace*. Sisters, OR: Multnomah Publishers, Inc., 1995.

Stanley, Charles. *The Wonderful Spirit-Filled Life*. Nashville, TN: Oliver-Nelson Books, 1992.

About the Author

James P. Gills, M.D., is founder and director of St. Luke's Cataract and Laser Institute in Tarpon Springs, Florida. Internationally respected as a cataract surgeon, Dr. Gills has performed more cataract extractions with lens implantations than anyone else in the world. He has pioneered many advancements in the field of ophthalmology to make cataract surgery safer and easier.

As a world-renowned ophthalmologist, Dr. Gills has received innumerable medical and educational awards, highlighted by 1994–2004 listings in *The Best Doctors in America*. Dr. Gills is a clinical professor of ophthalmology at The University of South Florida, and was named one of the Best Ophthalmologists in America in 1996 by ophthalmic academic leaders nationwide. He has served on the Board of Directors of the American College of Eye Surgeons, the Board of Visitors at Duke University Medical Center, and the Advisory Board of Wilmer Ophthalmological Institute at Johns Hopkins University. He has published more than 185 medical papers and authored nine medical textbooks. Listed in Marquis' *Who's Who in America*, Dr. Gills was Entrepreneur of the Year 1990 for the State of Florida, received the Tampa Bay Business Hall of Fame Award in 1993 and the Tampa Bay Ethics Award from the University of Tampa in 1995. In 1996 he was awarded the prestigious Innovators Award by his colleagues in the American Society of Cataract and Refractive Surgeons. In 2000 he was presented with the Florida Enterprise Medal by the Merchants Association of Florida, named Humanitarian of the Year by the Golda Meir/Kent Jewish Center in Clearwater, and Free Enterpriser of the Year by the Florida Council on Economic Education. In 2001 The Salvation Army presented Dr. Gills their prestigious "Others" Award in honor of his lifelong commitment to service and caring.

Virginia Polytechnic Institute, Dr. Gills' alma mater, presented their University Distinguished Achievement Award to him in 2003. In that same year, Dr. Gills was appointed by Governor Jeb Bush to the Board of Directors of the Florida

Sports Foundation. In 2004 Dr. Gills was invited to join the prestigious Florida Council of 100, an advisory committee reporting directly to the governor on various aspects of Florida public policy affecting the quality of life and economic well-being of all Floridians.

While Dr. Gills has many accomplishments and varied interests, his primary focus is to restore physical vision to patients and bring spiritual enlightenment through his life. Guided by his strong and enduring faith in Jesus Christ, he seeks to encourage and comfort the patients who come to St. Luke's and to share his faith whenever possible. It was through sharing his insights with patients that he initially began writing on Christian topics. An avid student of the Bible for many years, he now has authored seventeen books on Christian living, with over five million in print. With the exception of the Bible, Dr. Gills' books are the most widely requested books in the U.S. prison system. In addition, Dr. Gills has published more than 185 medical articles and authored or coauthored nine medical reference textbooks. Five of those books were best-sellers at the American Academy of Ophthalmology annual meetings.

As an ultra-distance athlete, Dr. Gills participated in forty-six marathons, including eighteen Boston Marathons and fourteen 100-mile mountain runs. In addition, he completed five Ironman Triathlons in Hawaii and six Double Iron Triathlons. Dr. Gills has served on the National Board of Directors of the Fellowship of Christian Athletes and in 1991 was the first recipient of their Tom Landry Award.

Married in 1962, Dr. Gills and his wife, Heather, have raised two children, Shea and Pit. Shea Gills Grundy, a former attorney now full-time mom, is a graduate of Vanderbilt University and Emory University Law School. She and husband Shane Grundy, M.D. presented the Gills with their first grandchildren—twins, Maggie and Braddock.

They have since been joined by Jimmy Gills and Lily Grace. The Gills' son, J. Pit Gills, M.D., ophthalmologist, received his medical degree from Duke University Medical Center and in 2001 joined the St. Luke's staff. "Dr. Pit" and his wife, Joy, are the proud parents of Pitzer and Parker.

OTHER BOOKS BY JAMES P. GILLS, M.D.

LOVE: FULFILLING THE ULTIMATE QUEST
A quick refresher course on the meaning and method of God's great gift.
ISBN 0-88419-933-9

A BIBLICAL ECONOMICS MANIFESTO
(with Ronald H. Nash, Ph.D.)
How the best understanding of economics conforms with what the Bible
teaches on the subject.
ISBN 0-88419-871-5

THE UNSEEN ESSENTIAL: A STORY FOR OUR TROUBLED TIMES
A compelling, contemporary novel about one man's struggle to grow into
God's kind of love.
ISBN 1-879938-05-7

TENDER JOURNEY: A CONTINUING STORY FOR OUR TROUBLED TIMES
The long-awaited sequel to *The Unseen Essential.*
ISBN 1-8779938-17-0

COME UNTO ME: REFLECTIONS FROM THE WILDERNESS
Inspired by Dr. Gills's trip to the Holy Land, this book explores God's eter-
nal desire for mankind to get to know Him intimately.
ISBN 1-59185-214-5

TEMPLE MAINTENANCE: EXCELLENCE WITH LOVE
A how-to book for achieving lifelong total fitness of body, mind and spirit.
ISBN 1-879938-01-4

THE DYNAMICS OF WORSHIP
Designed to rekindle the heart with a passionate love for God. Gives the
who, what, when, where, why and how of worship.
ISBN 1-59185-657-4

THE PRAYERFUL SPIRIT: PASSION FOR GOD, COMPASSION FOR PEOPLE
Tells how prayer has changed Dr. Gills's life, the lives of patients and other
doctors.
ISBN 1-59185-215-3

BELIEVE AND REJOICE: CHANGED BY FAITH, FILLED WITH JOY
How faith in God can let us see His heart of joy.
ISBN 1-59185-608-6

IMAGINATIONS: MORE THAN YOU THINK
How focusing our thoughts will help us grow closer to God.
ISBN 1-59185-609-4

GOD'S PRESCRIPTION FOR HEALING: FIVE DIVINE GIFTS OF HEALING
The prescription for all your healing has already been designed within you
by your Creator. By faith you will come to know His purpose for your life,
your suffering, and your healing.
ISBN 1-59185-286-2

DARWINISM UNDER THE MICROSCOPE: HOW RECENT SCIENTIFIC
EVIDENCE POINTS TO DIVINE DESIGN
Lays a scientific foundation for "divine design" and equips the reader to
discuss the topic intelligently.

ISBN 0-88419-925-8

SPIRITUAL BLINDNESS
Learn to remove the obstructions to spiritual sight and clearly see the evidence of God's love and wisdom demonstrated everywhere in our world.

ISBN 1-59185-607-8

TRANSFORM YOUR MARRIAGE
An elegant 4- by 8.5-inch booklet to help couples develop new closeness
with each other and with the Lord.

ISBN 1-879938-11-1

THE WORRY DISEASE
Worry is a sign that we no longer truly believe in God. Rather than attempting to do things our own way, we must trust in the Lord and believe with
our hearts.

Pamphlet

DID YOU ENJOY THIS BOOK?

Dr. and Mrs. James P. Gills would love to hear from you!
Please let them know if *Rx for Worry: A Thankful Heart* has had
an effect in your life or in the lives of your loved ones. Send your
letters to:

St. Luke's Cataract and Laser Institute
P.O. Box 5000
Tarpon Springs, FL 34688-5000
Telephone: (727) 938-2020, Ext. 2200
            (800) 282-9905, Ext. 2200
Fax: (727) 372-3605